Turn Your Website Into a Lead Machine

Learn about your visitors/buyers and their behavior on your site, and design a successful website experience that will generate tons of leads.

By Rajib Roy

Copyright

Acknowledgments

I am extremely thankful to the team who worked closely with me in writing this book. Without their help, it would not have been possible for me to publish this book. As I am passing through a very busy time in my life, under normal circumstances it would have been insurmountably tough for me to sit down and write 300 pages as quickly as we have. But my incredible team was there for every step of the way, helping me to elaborate my ideas and write them down into this book, pasteurizing my concepts and knowledge like never before.

I would also like to thank my Editor **Shams Mohammed**, who spent several days and nights making this book perfect and readable.

My tremendous thanks to Hari Ramakrishnan, who helped to draw all the pictures used in this book, and to Tushar Kunda, who helped to design the beautiful cover.

Moreover, I want to thank my Royex team.

Table of Contents

Introduction

Statistics show that 95% of all websites out there are not well-designed enough to truly generate leads. Which category does your website fall under: the 5% of greatness, or the 95% of failure? If you currently find yourself among this 95% who could stand to make some improvements, then this book is absolutely the answer you've been looking for! The text within will show you exactly how to generate enough leads, and after reading this book, you will be able to successfully and handily transition yourself from the regular old 95% crowd into the elite 5%.

Naturally, lead generation is no easy feat. When I first started my business, I tried out a lot of lead generation methods, and most of those were failed to generate anything worthwhile. Through a period of learning and extensive trial and error, however, my business now consistently generates leads without any ads - while most businesses are still out there struggling to bring in leads with paid ads!

Once your website begins generating leads, the whole scenario will change. When you have enough leads, you can dictate the price, and this gives you a lot of freedom to do more things. You can choose and prioritize your leads, only considering the ones that have a future.

In his book *Outlier,* accomplished author Malcolm Gladwell says that he believes it takes 10,000 hours to become an expert in something – and I believe this wholeheartedly! I have been designing and developing websites for the last 17 years, and in total, my working hours in this field have certainly exceeded 10,000 hours. So I definitely consider myself an expert; and as an expert, in these pages, I am going to guide you through the whole process for making profitable, high-profile websites for your business.

 With this unique guide, you can learn precisely how to use your own website to increase your sales and profits!

Turn Your Website into a Lead Machine is going to give you all the information and advice that you need to successfully convert traffic into leads.

All the tips and tricks written in this incredible book are very easy to understand, as well, so you can immediately begin applying them to your website right after reading this guide.

If you are facing any of the following issues:

- o You have good traffic on your website, but the number of leads or online sales you get is very small.

Website bounce back numbers are very high.

- o People are not staying on your site long enough.
- o You have low traffic from Google organic searches.

… then this book is for you.

Within this book, you will learn:

- o How to turn your website into a strategic, powerful internet marketing and website sales tool that helps you to reach your target market and influence them to take action.
- o How to design your website, so that you can establish your authority and target specific internet traffic.
- o How to build a lead generation website to convert traffic into leads.
- o About the modern buyer's journey – and, based on that journey, how to design your website and write content for it.

No matter which niche market your business or organization supports, your visitors will now feel confident and comfortable in their decision to move forward and do business with you, after visiting your website.

Whether you've just started your business and this is your first website, or you are simply looking for strategies and new ways to recharge your business through your current website, this book is going to be perfect for you. In this guide, I'm going to give you a basic understanding of the whole process of lead generation; so, instead of simply including some tips for making a good and effective website, I've also tried to explain different topics for your knowledge. With that in mind, please don't skip any chapters.

Our first chapter describes the process of getting to know the buyer. But for that, of course, you first need to know what you're selling! In this section, I explain how you can choose the product/service that you want to sell by considering a few factors. Once you have determined them, you can then focus on your buyer. This involves defining and identifying your target market and then finally reaching out to them. In the next section, I describe how you can research your audience and effectively segment your target market.

The second chapter extends the focus to buyers, as to how they discovered/got to your website. I explain the three primary ways in which buyers find their way to your website, as well as how this influences their navigation patterns.

In the third chapter, we'll explore the reasons for your website's inability to generate leads. There are three primary issues - trust, traffic, and sales issues - coupled with other issues. We go into great detail highlighting the various reasons why your website might currently be failing to be a lead magnet.

The fourth chapter contains a complete rundown of the things you need to know before you design your website is listed. The first section is based on Search Engine Optimization; you will learn what it is, why it matters, the factors that affect it, and become familiar with its different types. The next section talks about digital marketing, and how it can benefit your website. There is also a digital marketing strategy that you can implement into your website included. The third section highlights the importance of landing pages, as well as how to design one. The final section describes UI and UX design, and how you can improve it to increase your conversions.

The fifth chapter is all about website content. I explain how it serves as the cornerstone of any website, and how to create content based on the stage of the buyer's journey. The next section serves to follow up on that, with unique content ideas for the stages and steps, to create an engaging buyer's journey. You will learn all about different types of content on a website, and the secret to writing good content!

In the sixth chapter, I describe the process of a website redesign strategy. Beginning with the importance of redesign strategy, I list four different strategies based on your traffic source: SEO, social media, paid traffic, and direct traffic.

The seventh chapter is focused on the things you need to consider for website design and is followed up by the best design practices for designing and creating the various pages of your website. These pages include the homepage, about us, contact us, portfolio, product, service,

cart, checkout, thank you, search results, landing, blog landing and details, case study, career, and ebook pages.

The eighth and the final chapter starts with the three important automation features for your website: abandoned cart email, sequential email, and auto-follow up. The next section covers some tips to generate leads by improving your website's user experience. The final section lists out the three winning strategies that you can use to effectively increase your leads - repeat customers, retargeting, and free tools.

Chapter 1

Product, Leads & Buyers

Let's start by familiarizing you with products, leads, and buyers. The very first step to tackle here is determining what you are going to sell. What kind of product or service are you interested in offering to your customers?

You also need to learn how to price your products and services based on several factors. Next, you'll learn about website traffic and leads - and then, once you know that, you can proceed to learn about your buyers!

I'm going to explain how you can identify your target market and segment them based on certain criteria. You will learn what buyer personas are, and how you can curate them for your business. I'm also going to introduce you to the three-step buyer journey, and how customers buy based on the source of traffic.

What Are You Selling?

The very first step to running your online business is knowing what you are going to offer through your website. This can be broadly classified into two things: products and services. Products are tangible objects that you can touch and feel, and can be classified into numerous other categories depending on their criteria. Services, on the other hand, are transactions in which no physical goods are exchanged between the buyer and the seller.

If you have an eCommerce website, you are in a unique position where you can sell both products *and* services, or anyone of them. Here, you must determine what you want to sell to your buyers, and your website needs to be naturally centered around the product or service that you want to sell.

It is not always obvious to sell directly through websites - take our website, Royex.ae, for example, we are selling different services, but people can't order directly from the website, as our service is complicated, and we need to sit down with customers to make sure we all understand the project details and the price, which also depends on the functionality of the projects. So, we collect leads from customers through our website. The customers then come to our website and, using our webform, they can then send us an email expressing their interest in developing a project through us.

Of course, if you're trying to become the next Amazon or Best Buy, you're going to need a massive budget! These are companies that have thousands of categories of countless products, targeting all kinds of customers. But unless you have all that extra money lying around, you're going to need to pinpoint the exact product or service that you are interested in offering. Everything else comes after that!

First things first: you need to list out all your products or services, and then organize them into categories. For example: if you want to run an online electronics store, you should set up categories there like "Mobile Phones", "Computer Accessories", "Home Appliances", etc.

Essentially, you need to be aware of what you are selling. So... what are you going to sell? It's a simple question, but also the most difficult to answer while starting a business. My background is in software development, and while I may have the skills to write code and build a software system from scratch... none of this is going to help me answer this question!

So, to answer my query and decide what type of software really sells in the industry, I began doing some market research. To accomplish this, I keenly observed a successful company, looking to understand what kind of service they provide – and this seems like an excellent start to understanding what products (software systems, in my case) you can build, and the services you can provide to your future customers.

Try to find what kind of service or product you are going to sell. Our company has a dedicated online portal, "royex.store", for this very purpose, where we have all our software products like mobile apps, E-books, etc. available for sale. Before developing any product, we first publish a short description of the new product on our website and then gather public opinions about it.

In some cases, we'll even offer pre-bookings to potential customers. Doing this allows us to understand the market for that product, and also helps us to decide whether we should proceed further. And if it ever happens that we get negative reviews, or there is insufficient interest in re-bookings, we can cancel our development plans and save resources to be invested in more profitable projects.

So, once you have decided to develop a product, you should always make sure that there is a sufficient market for it, and that it's going to sell. Do some market research, and gather people's opinions and thoughts about it. Once you are fully satisfied that there is a public demand for the product, you can proceed with development.

Factors to consider when selecting your product/service

1. **Understand your capabilities:** You need to understand your capabilities, regarding what you can build or sell - you must have a thorough understanding of what you can and cannot do.

2. **Follow your competitor:** Most of the time, observing your competitors is going to give you a very good idea of current market trends. I always try and learn from my competitors, building and improving my products based on the competition's activities.

3. **Understand your Market Access:** You should equip yourself with a very good understanding of your target market. You need to access which niche you want to approach and then build your product accordingly. This will help you to gain a good foothold when entering the industry.

> *"It makes sense to find and know your market, and then create a product for it, rather than create a product you love and figure out no one is looking for it."*

4. Manpower availability: Once you've started a business, you need to hire the necessary amount of manpower to assist you. Therefore, you must have a good knowledge of the skill set and skill level of the available workforce that you have. This also follows through the fact that any decision you make regarding the product type also has to incorporate that available skill set. For example, if you have decided to produce a software system in a particular programming language, you also need to be sure that you have developers available who are adept in this language.

Product or Service line up

This is a crucial concept in the business plan. Once you have decided on which product/service you want to sell, you also need to decide what kind of follow-up products/services you can offer to your customers. These will greatly help in repeat business from the same customer, as well as work to attract new customers, as people nowadays generally prefer to obtain all their related services from the same place. By setting up those options, this effectively saves both parties valuable time and money, while at the same time building a very strong customer relationship.

One fine example of this concept is performing Website Development for a client. Alongside this service, you could also offer them Search Engine Optimization, Website Maintenance, and Website Hosting. In most cases, this will be a customized package for the client, as they can pick and choose from amongst the additional services (also known as a product or service line-up) that best suits their needs. This package can include all of the additional services or a custom combination of them.

Below, you'll find some examples of the additional services that can be offered to potential clients, supplemental to the main service.

Main Service	1st Lineup Services
Website Development	Search Engine Optimization Website Maintenance Website Hosting Web Security Testing
Search Engine Optimization	Website Maintenance Social Media Marketing Website Redesign
Mobile Application Development	App Performance Test App Page Optimization Mobile App Marketing

This list is just one example of the kinds of follow-up services you can offer. In some cases, the client might even just opt for a small service like SEO, and then include additional services as it suits them.

When a client initially comes to you for a specific service, you can offer them additional services at the same time; and in this scenario, the package price would be set accordingly. In some cases, however, this increase in cost might drive away potential customers - so it is always better to assess each client first, and then discuss the package accordingly.

In some instances, it might also be more beneficial for you to capture a client for only one service, initially. Once the main project has been completed, you might offer additional services, usually at a premium, to follow-up with the main product. The great advantage of this approach is that the client has now already seen your performance with the main project and, if they're satisfied, will likely be more open and willing to try out the additional service as well. Once you have captured the attention of your customers with high-quality products and services, it is very easy to retain them and to generate repeat sales from them through additional services, however small each one may seem.

Once we get a lead from a client, we'll try to find out the potential sales amount. Let's say that a client comes to us for Mobile Apps Development (price is $20K) and that Mobile Apps development is the main service. In the future, then, we can also offer them Apps Performance Tests ($5K), Apps Page Optimization ($10K), and Mobile Apps Marketing ($20K).

With this in mind, our potential sales amount is $20K + $5K + $10K + $20K = $55k USD – and so, the client's value in our CRM is actually $55K, not $20K! Sometimes, we'll even give a discount on our main service, as we believe we will get enough money from them in the future. If we've given someone a 25% discount on our main service (Mobile Apps Development), our potential sales amount is still $50K, which is good enough for us.

To fully maximize your profit, you need to have a good collection of products for your first lineup. Companies need to invest in marketing, as well as in gaining new potential customers and ensuring that they go ahead with their purchases, which will increase your business. This is usually a one-time cost of capturing a customer for the main service; after that, the first lineup services are generated automatically.

In one real-life case, we were given a project to develop a website for a TV channel. It was a popular channel, preferred by around 40% of the public, and this gave us a unique opportunity to reach a lot of people and promote our brand.

When the project was completed, the CEO of the channel was extremely satisfied with the performance. We offered them additional services of mobile apps, microsite development, and SEO; and since we had already proven our quality of services to them, the CEO agreed and opted for all three additional products! So we were able to generate fantastic repeat sales from a very satisfied customer.

What is the price of your product/service?

Let me dispel a myth or two about pricing. Price is not the consumer's biggest concern. It's at the very end of the list of reasons why people don't buy! Customers like to purchase products and services that are highly-priced.

Whatever the case, though, if the price is open, it must be competitive. But if the price is not open, you suggest a custom price, and then the price depends on the customer, not the products. You have to understand what kind of customer you're dealing with, as well as their maximum purchasing limit.

"If the price is not open, then the price depends on the customer, not the products."

Although your prospects may initially object to high prices verbally, there may be other thoughts going around in their mind, such as:

- o Is this right?
- o Is there anything better than that?
- o Is this the right suggestion?
- o Will this solve our problem?
- o Is my team going to use it?
- o What else will I think about buying this?

- o Is this something that I'll use and enjoy?
- o Will this organization look after me and represent us?
- o Am I better off buying another thing?
- o Will there be something better available next week?
- o Do I have all the information?
- o Will this be a mistake, like past decisions?

When these aspects have been dealt with to the customer's satisfaction, then the price will no longer be the issue.

Here, I'm going to try to explain a few factors you need to consider for pricing because it is critical to your success that your product/service is priced correctly. Before we do that, though, we need to consider the following factors for pricing…

Factors for setting the right price

"There are many ways of determining the right price," … "Nonetheless, successful companies use a variety of resources and recognize that your client is always the key factor to consider. The more you learn about your customers, the more you can give them the value they want, and the more you can charge."

Know Your Customer

To know and understand your consumer, it is important to conduct some kind of market research. This endeavor can range from informal inspections of your existing customer base (which you send out in an email, coupled with some nice promotions) to extensive (and potentially costly) research projects carried out by third-party consultancies. Market research firms should analyze the market and very granularly segment your potential customers by demographics, purchasing, pricing, etc. If you don't have several thousand dollars to spend on market research, you can just look at consumers in several different groups - the budgetary sensitivity, convenience-focused, and those to whom status is important. Figure out which segment and price you are targeting accordingly.

Know Your Costs

A fundamental principle of pricing is that you have to cover your costs, and then make a profit. Naturally, this means that you must know how much your product costs. You must also consider how much you have to price the commodity, along with how many you have to sell to make a profit.

Remember that the cost of a commodity is greater than the actual cost of the item; overhead costs are also included here, which may include fixed costs (such as rent) and variable expenses (such as shipping or storage fees). These costs must be included in your estimate of the actual cost of your product.

"Come up with X first. X is your cost of raw materials, labor, rent, and everything it took to make the product so that if you sold it, you would break even," … "Y becomes what you think you need to make on it. That may depend on your business. Restaurants, overall, make about 4%, which is pretty low. If you want 10%, then you factor that into your costs, and that is what you charge."

Many businesses either don't factor in all their costs and underprice, or they literally factor in all their costs and then expect to make a profit with one product, and therefore overcharge. A good rule of thumb for this is to make a spreadsheet of all the costs you need to cover each month, which might include the following:

o Your actual product costs, including labor and the costs of marketing and selling those products.
o All of the operating expenses necessary to own and operate the business.
o The costs associated with borrowing money (debt service costs).
o Your salary as the owner and/or manager of the business.

o A return on the capital that you and any other owners or shareholders have invested.

o Capital for future expansion and replacement of fixed assets as they age.

o List the dollar amount for each on your spreadsheet. The total should give you a good idea of the gross revenues you will need to generate, to ensure that you cover all those costs.

Know Your Revenue Target

You should also have an income target of how much you want your company to profit. Take that sales target, add to your development, marketing, and marketing costs, and you can then find a price per product that you want to charge. It's a simple process if you have only one thing: estimate the number of units you expect to sell for the next year, break your sales goal down by the number of units you expect to sell, and you'll now have the price you need to sell your product at, to meet your income and revenue targets.

If you have several different items, you will divide the total revenue goal by each category. Then, make the same approximation to the price that each commodity must be priced at, to meet all the financial objectives.

Know Your Competition

It is also extremely helpful and insightful to look at the market – after all, the company competing against you would probably do the same thing. Are the products they have available compared to yours? If so, you can actually use their pricing as an initial indicator, and then see if your product has an extra value; do you offer an additional benefit, for example, with your goods, or are your goods considered to be of higher quality? If so, then maybe you will be able to support a higher price! Be vigilant about regional differences and always bear your costs in mind, though. In this case, the main thing is to compare net prices, and not just the list price (or reported price). Such information can be obtained through telephone calls, hidden shopping, published information, etc. Throughout his phase of your research, remember how the business and goods - and the competition - are viewed by the consumer. Be brutally honest with your assessment.

Know Where the Market Is Headed

You may not be a fortune teller, but luckily, you can still track external factors that will have an impact on the future demand for your company. These factors can range from simple weather patterns to legislation that could impact your products' future sales. Take your competitors (and their actions) into account. Will a competitor respond to your introduction of a new product by engaging your company in a price war?

Whether you offer products or services, you need certain pages on your website, such as testimonials, a portfolio, reviews, and a product/service page. I'm going to discuss each of these individually, later on.

Your pricing strategy, features, benefits, marketing strategies, and your website visuals will depend on your product/service choice. It is much easier to make your website successful when you have a clear understanding of your products/services. If you do not do this, you will not be able to determine who your buyers will be - which I will discuss in a later chapter.

What is Traffic and What is a Lead?

Web traffic simply refers to the number of users who visit a website during a particular time. For example, if 300 people visited your website in one day, then your daily traffic for that day equals 300.

From the web traffic, those users that follow the call to action are referred to as leads. If you're running a business website, the number of leads you generate is a far more important metric than your website's traffic.

A lead is, in simple terms, a person or an agency that has an interest in what you are offering to sell. Leads can be created for reasons such as list creation, the acquisition of e-newsletter lists, or sales leads. Strategies for producing leads typically fall under the category of "advertisement", but may also involve unpaid outlets, such as organic search engine results gained from Search Engine Optimization or recommendations from existing customers.

Leads may come from various channels or events, i.e. via the Internet, personal contacts, clients, telemarketers, telephone calls, and advertisers. Lead generation is often combined with the management of leads to pass through the purchasing funnel. The term "pipeline marketing" applies to this mix of operations.

A person is typically assigned a lead to follow-up on. Once the user (e.g. salesperson) checks and qualifies it to have potential business, then the lead is turned into a business opportunity. This opportunity then has to go through multiple sales stages before the contract has finally been secured.

"A lead is, in simple terms, a person or an agency that has an interest in what you are offering to sell."

Marketing Leads and Sales Leads

A lead is typically the contact information and, in some situations, the demographic information of a person interested in a certain product or service. In the market for lead generation, you'll find two forms of leads: business leads and marketing leads.

Sales leads are created based on demographic factors, such as FICO score, employment, sex, income in households, etc. Such leads are resold to several advertisers, and selling leads are usually followed up by the sales force, via phone calls.

Sales leads are frequently found in the mortgage, loan, and banking industries.

Marketing leads are brand-specific leads for a specific advertiser offer and are offered only once, standing in direct contrast to sales leads. Due to the need for transparency to generate marketing leads, marketing lead campaigns can be optimized by mapping leads to their sources. For example, if you were looking to advertise a mobile app, then you would target mobile users rather than desktop users.

An investor lead is more of a sales lead type of thing. An investor lead is the name of an individual or entity that is possibly interested in participating in investment and constitutes the first step of a process of selling an investment.

Investor leads are known to have some degree of disposable income they're able to use in the interest of partaking in acceptable investment opportunities – whether that be in the form of interest, dividend, profit-sharing, or wealth growth in exchange for return on investments.

Investor lead lists are usually created by investment polls, investor newsletter subscriptions, or companies raising capital and selling the database of people who have expressed interest in their opportunity.

Investor lead lists are widely used by small businesses that are seeking to fund an investment, or simply require growth funding that was not already readily available from banks and other traditional sources of financing.

Good Leads and Bad Leads

Working to ensure that your leads are of a certain consistency is essential in maintaining a healthy business with lead generation. To a lead buyer, nothing is more annoying than searching for poor leads! This is not only a drain on the business's resources, but it also has the potential to adversely affect the perceived value of your leads, in the customer's eyes. And how can you spot the difference between genuinely good and bad leads?

One of the most important skills needed for lead generation is being able to differentiate the good from the bad. A lot of time is lost when it comes to managing the selling pipeline and seeking opportunities that turn out to be pointless.

Quality lead production is one of the largest challenges that businesses face. If your messaging is too ambiguous, your scope too broad, or your approach too violent, it can easily cost you bad leads. Once you've discovered papers documenting the billions of US dollars lost due to bad data and inadequate lead generation strategies, you don't have to look too hard.

But beyond basic economics, bad leads can also harm the company itself, as they can effectively damage the customer experience. With efforts focused on the wrong buyers, flagging behind can be easy for the level of customer service and aftercare.

"The secret to business growth and success is being able to tell whether a lead is worth pursuing."

Here's a roadmap for telling the good quality leads apart from the weaker ones:

Real leads are the most profitable, and being careful in determining what qualifies will help you to boost your conversion rates. Capable leads need your company now, have shown confidence in you as a brand, and have the budget to buy them.

This does not mean that suspects and prospects are not worth your time, though. A target very well may already be interested in a particular type of product or service, and is already engaging with you (such as signing up for your newsletter)!

Suspects might be people who just follow you on social media, but who have not yet shared their info with you. As it turns out, they are interested in what you know, not what you sell. And this is exactly where your product promotion comes in. Blogs are a key part of any marketing plan and can turn suspects into prospects, and prospects into actual leads.

Who are the Buyers?

This step is crucial because without knowing who is going to buy your products/services, you cannot make your website a selling machine. You might offer the best quality products or top-of-the-line service... but if you can't reach out to potential buyers, or they can't find you, then your business will eventually fail.

Your website design should match your buyer persona. If your buyer doesn't like your website, then they will not buy from you. Simple as that. For comparison, picture a website that sells Omega watches, and then another one that sells non-branded, cheap watches. Both watches show you the time, but these two buyer levels are not the same. The buyer who will use Omega will never use non-branded watches, and those who are using non-branded watches can't afford to buy Omega. And so, these websites can't be the same, either. This is why knowing who your buyers are so important!

Before starting the selling process, determining where your potential buyer will come from will put you ahead of the game. Know who your buyer is.

When you have decided which product or service you want to sell, your next step is going to be gaining a good understanding of your target market. Your chosen target market is the group of people that you want to sell your products or services to – and when you have identified them, you need to work on how to *connect* with them so that you can sell your product.

Defining your target market is one of the most important tasks for a business owner. It is the cornerstone of all elements in your marketing strategy, from designing and naming your products or services to support the marketing channels that you use.

It should be noted that you cannot just opt to vaguely include everybody in your target audience. You need to be specific about which group of individuals to target for selling.

Once you have a very good understanding of your target market, though, you will then be able to concentrate your advertising, material, promotional languages, and focus only on reaching the audience that will most likely become clients. Armed with your deep insight into your audience, you will begin to see higher conversion rates and better ROI (Return on Investment) – key measurements of importance to any marketer!

Knowing exactly who your target audience is, is one of the absolute most important factors for success. I try to observe my chosen target market very keenly, to understand their behavior, buying preferences, their social and business circles, etc. Using this knowledge, I can predict which products they will search for and which platforms they will use, and this will help me inappropriately placing my product advertisement so that they can see and contact me. Once contact is established, it becomes easier to seal the deal for the product.

Now, I'm going to take you through a simple process, helping you to understand who communicates with your organization and competitors, and then using that knowledge to create a clear target audience when developing your brand. It's all about focusing, while at the same time expanding your reach.

Target Market Definition

The particular group of people you wish to reach with your advertising message for potential sales is your target market. These are the people who buy your products or services the most often, and who are bound together by some common features, such as demographics and behaviors.

The clearer you define your target group, the better you can understand how and where you can obtain the best outlook. You can start this process with large categories, such as youngsters or single dads, but you have to get a lot closer to the best possible conversion rates.

Be sure to keep in mind that, by defining your target market, you are not excluding everyone else from your potential customers - everyone can still buy from you. You are just focusing on your advertisement strategy.

Your target market should be based on actual public polling, not simply a feeling of well-being. You must be willing to learn while you are traveling, adapt, and obey the people who want to buy from you - even if they are not necessarily the customers you were going to reach initially.

Back when I originally started selling my product, I did not identify any target market; I just tried to market my product to everybody, and as a result, I failed to get any positive sales. This led to frustration, as all my efforts were in vain.

But after thinking it over and doing the proper research, I was able to identify that I should only focus on potential customers from the Middle East (UAE, Bahrain, KSA, etc.) and that I should not waste my time or resources on making sales in other Asian countries. The reason for this was that Asian countries tend to have a lot more local software developer options, at much cheaper rates, and it was therefore highly unlikely that any of them would go for a Dubai-based company instead.

This new understanding helped me begin focusing my efforts on my target market. And while we certainly do have some Asian clients, they account for only 5% of our total sales. Now we have a filtering procedure for Asian clients before we engage in any further dealing.

"These are the people who buy your products or services the most often, and who are bound together by some common features…"

Identifying Your Current Target Market

Defining your target market is just identifying who you're trying to sell to. It all starts with your current customers. Ask yourself (or better yet, ask your customers, if you have them) some key questions:

- o Are they mainly men or women?
- o What are their ages?
- o Married, single, engaged?
- o Where do they live?
- o What's their income (or budget for your product)?
- o What types of content do they like to consume? Blogs, videos, podcasts?
- o What social media channels do they use? How often?
- o What do they do in their free time? Workout? Watch TV? Go to events? Shop?

Speaking to Your Target Market

Now that you have a picture of your target market, you can start effectively marketing to their specific needs! For example, if you're looking to sell clothing to moms that are juggling kids and a job, then perhaps shorter, 30-seconds-long videos or podcasts they can listen to are better ways to reach them than something more traditional and time-consuming, like longer blogs.

You know they like Facebook, so you can concentrate your ads and content on that platform. And because clothing is so visual, of course, you want to make sure that your website is easy to navigate and has lots of great pictures of your products.

How to Conduct Audience Research

Compile data on your current customers

A great first step for finding out who wants to purchase more from you is to find out who uses your products or services. If you have only recently started your business, you can still get a good initial idea of this by finding out more about your competitor's customers.

Once you understand the characteristics of your existing customer base, you can find more people that match the same mold. You can do this by conducting surveys and asking people to complete questionnaires. Do not include too many questions, however, because this may discourage people from participating and giving you any useful information.

You can prepare a database to collect information about your customers. Some basic information that you can collect is:

Age: You do not need to know an exact age; a rough age range will be quite useful for you, as you look to prepare your marketing strategy.

Location (and time zone): Where in the world do your existing customers live? Aside from understanding which geographical areas to target, you can also find out what hours are the most important for your customer service and sales representatives to be online, as well as when your social ads and posts should be scheduled, to make sure you ensure maximum visibility.

Language: Language is one of the biggest barriers in business. For ideal communication to take place, you need to be aware of the popular language amongst your customers.

Spending power and patterns: How much money will your current customers spend? How are sales in your price category approached? Do you have specific financial issues or preferences? All of these need to be considered, when dealing with your target audience.

Interests: What do your customers like to do? What television shows are they currently watching? Which other companies do they interact with? Knowing about these potential interests will be of great help in defining your audience's niche.

Stage of life: Is it likely that your customers are students? New parents? Parents of adolescents? Retreats?

If you sell B2B products/services, you will have a slightly different category. You may want to collect information about the size of companies from your corporate target market and the titles of the people who are making purchasing decisions. Are you looking for the CEO of marketing? The CTO? The head of social marketing? Knowing who you need to speak to within the business is a crucial first step in building your brand identity.

Consider my Royex Technologies company as an example: we have more than 300 customers. Out of those, 85% are consumers from GCC countries, 10% are from Europe, 2% are from other countries, and only 3% come from Asian countries. Therefore, we much concentrate on GCC customers and market our products/services to them. And since Arabic is the main language in those countries, we have added Arabic to our website. Besides, in our office, we have hired an Arabic speaker to specifically communicate with these clients in their native languages. This allows us to develop our business, and could only be done by evaluating our client information.

Look to the website and social media analytics

So, where do you get all this research information from your audience? Social media analysis can be a great way to fill the holes in your consumer analysis. You can also grasp who communicates with your social accounts, even if they are not customers yet!

Check out the competition

Once you have settled on your target audience and adjusted your advertising strategy, you should also consider what your competitors are doing.

Looking at what your competitors are up to, you might be able to answer a few key questions: do your competitors pursue the same segments of the market you do? Are they hitting segments you did previously not think about? How do you position yourself?

You will not be able to get detailed research from your audience about people interacting with your competitors, but you will be able to understand how they view themselves, and whether it allows them to make online interactions. This review should help you understand which markets they are targeting, as well as the success of their efforts.

Be clear about the value of your product or service

This is the key distinction between features and benefits for all marketers. You can sit there and list a product's features all day long, but no one is truly assured of buying it from you unless you can justify the advantages.

Functionality is what the product is or does. The advantages are the results. How can your product make your buyer's life easier, better, or more interesting?

If you do not have a clear list of your product's benefits, then it's time to start brainstorming! You will also automatically give some basic information about your demographic goal when making your benefit statements.

For example, if your service helps customers connect with qualified pet-sitters, you could already be quite convinced that your group is going to consist mainly of pet owners (and probably travelers) - and if your company allows people to remotely backup their mobile images, you know that you are targeting people who own mobile devices and who take lots of photos.

If you are not sure exactly how your goods are used to help consumers... why not ask them? You might even find that people are making and using your products or services for purposes that you did not even think of! This could change your perception of your target audience for future sales. An email survey can provide you with all manner of great insights, and you can also ask your social channels a quick question.

Create a target market statement

Now is the time to boil everything you have learned down to a simple statement that describes your target audience. This is your first step in developing a brand positioning message.

For the time being, let's stick to a statement that clearly defines your target market.

For example, this is the brand marketing statement for dubizzle.com: "Buy and sell anything in the UAE". We are interested in the last piece of that statement, which describes the objective market: UAE.

Try to incorporate the most important demographic and behavioral characteristics you have found when constructing your objective market statement. For example: "Our target market is the age of [gender], who live in [place or place type], and who like [activity]."

You do not necessarily need to stick to these specific identifiers. Gender might be irrelevant to your target customer, but three or four key behaviors can be incorporated into your statement. The ultimate aim here is to compile all your work into a simple statement that can help direct your marketing efforts.

If you offer multiple products or services, you may also need to create a target market statement for each product or category.

Test social ads on your target market

Now, it's time to have some fun and see how you can make research work for your target audience!

The first step is to create social advertisements specifically for the exact market that you just defined. You may have sufficient advertising material from a previous campaign or your organic social posts, but be true to yourself whether the content is as relevant as it should be.

Does the language speak with exactly the right voice to the market you have defined? In the background of your target market, do graphics make sense?

When you are pleased with your innovation, it is time for you to get to your target audience using social tools. This next step is very important because you're going to determine which social media platforms to use. See our statistics on demography for every social network, to see which information will better allow you to meet the demographic target that you have defined. For instance, in the UAE, Facebook is not perfect, but it is a great platform in India.

Once you have picked your channels, your ad and advertising targeting can be granular. Use the features identified in your target market statement to build an audience for your advertising and content. Social networks may vary slightly, but they tend to offer comprehensive targeting options – and if you need any further details before starting, take some time to research some guides on online marketing.

Track your advertising and content success, to see what kind of measurable results you achieve. Once you've set up a benchmark, you can use A/B research to learn more about the best marketing strategies, and whether you need to develop your creative approach to connect with your audience more directly.

Revisit your audience research as needed

The results of your test can give you additional insight when you first create your target market statement. Make sure to incorporate each lesson you learn and review your market statement regularly to ensure that your most valuable potential customers are still described accurately.

Keep in mind that your target market can also shift over time. For instance, back in the 1980s, Atari sold their gaming console to children. Today, Atari is targeting the same people who played their games in the 1980s - but these people are now 35 years old, and look back at Atari as a nostalgic part of their childhood, and not as a state-of-the-art gaming system.

Is your target audience too familiar? The right target market is an important factor for a profitable company. You need to spend time getting to know your market if you plan to make your company successful!

Segmenting Your Target Market

Your target market may not be one single area - it can be multiple. For example, we deal with website designing. In the modern era, almost every business out there goes for a good website to represent them. This means that both startups, as well as established big corporations, need website development and maintenance. And they both become part of our target markets, even though they both fall into separate categories.

It is necessary to segregate the target market into separate categories for various reasons. This segregation can be done based on current purchase capabilities, prospects, etc.

For example, a business that has just started up has a limited budget. They need to develop a website or a mobile app, but have not yet begun earning anything - or if they have, it is still only a negligible amount. Their spending budget is therefore very small, and naturally, you cannot charge them a high fee that they will not be able to afford. However, these businesses are present in large quantities, which increases the number of potential customers. Moreover, it is very easy to access the high ranking and decision-making people in these companies. So this is a very attractive market for us. All new startups, SMEs, individuals, and hobbyists fall into this category.

On the other hand, big corporate companies, government entities, groups of companies, etc. make up a separate category. These customers have a lot of money and a very high budget - however, it is not easy to secure their business. They also have a very high turnover rate, due to their ability to afford better offers.

One of our clients is Emaar, the company that constructed and developed Burj Khalifa, the world's tallest building. It is not easy to sell products to Emaar, and it is very tough to meet with the chairperson. Since you are not dealing with the main person directly, it takes a lot of time in the corporate culture for the completion of the approval process. Sometimes, it takes more than three months to complete a sales process in Dubai. But the value of these projects is much higher than if you were to sell the same kind of products/service to a startup - and the prospects from this kind of corporate company are also huge.

We have named these categories as "Startup Group" and "Corporate Group".

When you first start your business, you must work on the Startup group first. You can do a test of your products/services with this group, as the number of people in this group is quite high. This will help you to build your portfolio, and by selling products/services in this group you can take steps to make your company profitable. The whole cost structure can be developed based on the results of this category.

Once you have developed a good enough portfolio, and want to increase your company profit, you can then move on to the Corporate Group, which can help you to easily multiply your profit by up to five times.

Benefits of Startup Groups

- o The number of companies in this group is high
- o You can test your products/services
- o Easily accessible
- o Lead closing time is very fast
- o The payout time is also very fast
- o You can adapt your terms and conditions here

Disadvantages

- o Less profit
- o Huge Competition

o They may not complete the project (so try to get a big portion of the money in the first few rounds)

o There is no guarantee that they will give you repeat business in the future

Benefits of Corporate Groups

o Make you extremely profitable

o Your company stability will be high, as these companies will give you work regularly

o Improve your branding

o Strong portfolio

o Acquire more work through connections

Disadvantages:

o It's tough to close deals

o It takes time

o You need to follow their terms and conditions

o They usually process payments only after the work is complete. So, initially, you need to invest in the project

We have now worked on several small businesses in the Startups Group. Based on our learning and results, we can now move on to the Corporate Group.

It's always a good idea to have two such categories for your target market, with one group consisting of a large number of customers who are each paying low charges, while the other has very few clients, but the payments are high. These categories will balance off each other to give you consistent, good profits.

What is a Buyer Persona?

If you are even remotely familiar with marketing, you must have heard the term "buyer persona". This is quite an important subject, when it comes to buyers, even though it doesn't get the attention it deserves.

A buyer persona is a way of describing a target customer by creating a research-based profile. It depicts your ideal customers and important details, such as their habits, obstacles, and decision-making.

It's common to have multiple buyer personas for a business. For example, if the end-user of your product needs to gain the approval of others before making a purchase, each individual involved in that decision represents a separate persona. They'll have different criteria for evaluating your product, and you'll need different strategies for addressing those needs.

Buyer personas are sometimes called "customer" or "marketing" personas (or profiles) - but whichever term you use, the ultimate meaning and purpose are the same. Buyer personas help businesses understand and empathize with their customers so that they can do a better job of acquiring and serving them.

Buyer Personas are Important

Buyer personas aim to generate and serve customers based on their needs. It may seem simple, but in all reality, it is much more complicated than you might think.

Most companies are too focused on themselves, rather than catering to what the customer needs. This makes it challenging for them to understand buyer decisions.

Inclining towards businesses that you know and trust is an instinct for buyers when choosing a product or service. This trust can be earned by showing real concern and care for your customers. There is simply no other alternative.

So, the point I'm trying to make here is, you need to alter your way of presenting yourself, to build trust between you and your buyers. This change also has to be subtle, rather than a drastic one.

You can start by catering to your potential buyers' needs and issues. Once you do that, they will begin opening up to you, and seeing what you really have to offer.

This will also help you to create buyer personas, which can help you be on top of your customers' needs and, ultimately, guide your business.

How Do I Create a Buyer Persona for My Business?

You should involve both internal and external research for determining your buyer personas. As stated earlier, you also need multiple buyer personas, but you don't have to create them all simultaneously. This can be a slow process that evolves and adapts with time.

Start with one potential customer, and then create the persona based on available information. And then, as you conduct more research, make changes to the persona as needed.

You can start by preparing a list of questions to interview. Then, after researching, you can craft your persona. Try and make your persona at least a page long, to ensure that all the basic information is covered.

This isn't the final form for your persona, as you can always add more to it by interacting with customers, and asking them to take questionnaires and surveys. Thus, your persona will keep evolving as you continue to gather more information about your customers. The key here is to be patient and be insightful, and to keep your persona updated and accurate.

Example of a buyer persona

This is the buyer persona of Mr. Hamid, a resident of UAE:

Name: Mr. Hamid Yusuf

Age: 35

Gender: Male

Location: Dubai

Occupation: Accountant

Marital Status: Married for 4 years

Purchasing behavior:

Shopping: Likes to check the product offline before making an online purchase.

Purchasing: Does not like to purchase something owned by everyone. Likes to purchase high-quality products from overseas.

Online/mobile: Actively uses the internet and mobile browsing. Loves to browse Facebook in particular.

Media: Prefers magazines over TV.

From the above example, you can offer products based on Mr. Hamid's persona to make him your customer! We've learned that Mr. Hamid is someone who would love product samples because he likes to test products offline first. He also likes uncommon overseas products and products of high value – therefore, Facebook or targeted magazines may be the best way to get to him.

What is the Buyer's Journey?

"The buyer journey is nothing more than a series of questions that must be answered."

~ Michael Brenner

Buyers demand information about your product/service that they can't find online. They are not interested in being prospected or closed, as it doesn't add value to them.

To customize and personalize your sales process to cater to the buyer, you first need to understand what the buyer journey is. In this section, we're going to define the buyer's journey and show you how to think through it, when working prospects in your pipeline.

The buyer's journey is the process through which buyers undergo the steps to be aware, to consider, and decide to purchase a product or service.

The buyer's journey has three steps:

o   Awareness Stage: The buyer realizes that they have a problem/the stage where the buyer realizes there is a need or a problem.

o Consideration Stage: The buyer defines their problem and researches options to solve it/the stage where the buyer discusses and pinpoints their problem, and the researchers attempt to solve it.

o Decision Stage: The stage where the buyer makes a decision.

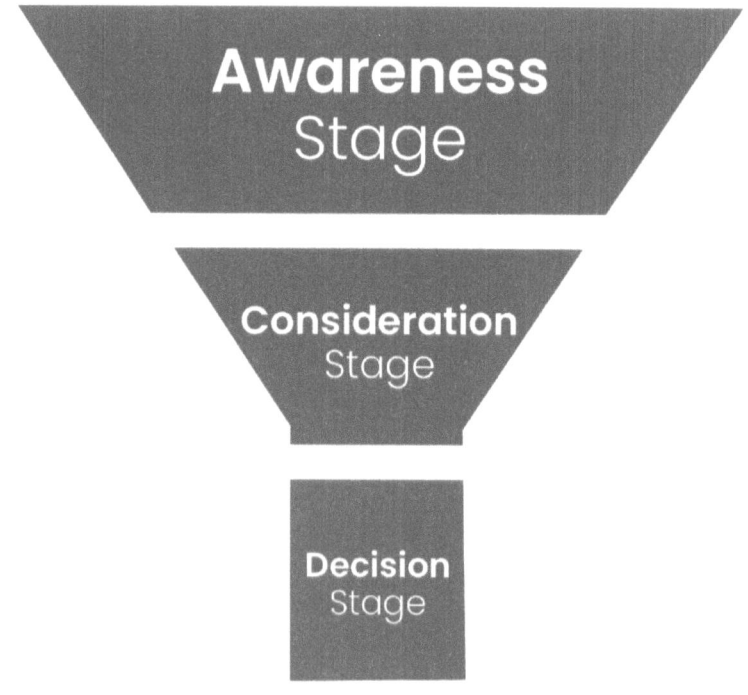

Images: Buyer's journey funnel

How to Define Your Company's Buyer's Journey

Interviewing your customers, prospects, and your team is a fantastic way to get to understand the buyer's journey. Doing this will help you understand your buyers on a closer level. Below, I have listed some questions (based on the stage of the buyer journey) that you should ask.

Awareness Stage

During the awareness stage, buyers try to identify their issues or challenges they face. They also seek out opportunities to pursue – and if this issue or opportunity is important to them, they make a decision. To effectively grasp the awareness stage for your buyer, you need to ask yourself these questions:

o   How do the buyers outline their issues and goals?

o   How are the buyers enlightening themselves on these issues and goals?

o   What happens when the buyers do nothing about it?

o   What are the buyers' common misunderstandings about these issues and goals?

o   How are the buyers deciding to prioritize an issue or a goal?

Consideration Stage

At this stage, the buyer knows their problems and goals and wants to do something about them. For this, they look forward to solving their issues and meeting their goals using the approaches that are available to them. You should ask yourself these questions:

o   What kind of solutions are buyers looking into?

o How are the buyers educating themselves on the different types of solutions?

o How are the buyers judging the benefits and risks of these types of solutions?

o What is the decision-making process of buyers, in choosing the right type of solution for them?

Decision Stage

In the Decision stage, buyers have already decided on a solution category. For example, they could write a pros/cons list of specific offerings and then decide on the one which best meets their needs. To define the Decision stage, questions you should ask yourself are:

o What criteria do buyers use, to evaluate the available offerings? How are the buyers judging the types of solutions available to them?

o What does the buyer like about your offer, compared to other offerings? What don't they like about your offering?

o Who should be involved in the decision-making process? How do their opinions on the decision vary?

o Does the buyer expect to try the solution before they purchase it?

o Are the buyers undertaking any strategies or implementing any plans outside of purchasing?

Once you have answers to these questions, you can understand the buyer's journey.

How Do Buyers Buy?

Not all buyers have the same buying behavior. As we learned in the previous section, not all the visitors who end up on your website end up there by looking up for it! Some discover your website through social media, some stumble upon an ad, etc. As such, there is also a difference in the ways that customers buy. Let's take a look at the three different ways that buyers buy from a website.

By searching for the product/service

This is the kind of buyer who actively searches for the product/service over the internet. They feel a demand for the product, and thus seek out methods to purchase it. For example, let's say a buyer urgently needs an internet router for his home. He is already aware of the product; he even knows the brand and the model that he wants to go for. He looks it up on the internet, to find the best deals for that router.

Upon searching, he finds that your website is offering the router he's looking for. He browses your website and sees that it fits all his criteria. Maybe he wasn't even aware of your website before today – but he then purchases the router from your website.

Compelled by social media

Here, the buyer had no intention of making a purchase or even visiting your website. Let's say you were just browsing Twitter, and you came across a tweet from your friend stating that he got tickets to a music concert in your area. You see similar posts of the concert tickets, as well as a link to purchase these tickets. Feeling compelled, you visit the link to find out more information about the concert.

You get excited, and purchase tickets for the show! You have purchased from a website, just like the man who searched for a router - but how is this different from the above case? See, you had no intention of visiting the website by yourself, let alone purchasing those tickets. You were influenced by social media and made an impulse purchase. Had it not been for the social media post, you would not have even searched for the concert tickets. Your purchase was a decision influenced by a third-party.

Direct purchase

This third and final kind of buyer is someone who is already aware of your website and of the products that you offer. He knows the URL of your website and enters it directly into the address bar to access your site. Both in this case and the first case, the buyers knew what they wanted beforehand - the difference lies in brand awareness.

In the first case, the buyer didn't know who to purchase from, but he knew the product that he wanted. He had to research who offered that router at the best price point. But, in this case, the buyer is already aware of your business, your products, and your pricing models. He visits your website directly and makes the purchase.

Chapter 2

Buyer's behavior on your website

Understanding buyer behavior is important for your website. You need to know how the buyer got there, and how they navigate your website. Usually, there are four sources of traffic to your website: direct, organic search, paid traffic, and social media.

You will learn more about each source of traffic here. You'll find that visitors from each traffic source tend to behave differently. You will also learn some tips on how to generate traffic for each of these sources in this chapter.

I have provided relevant examples for each buyer so that you can know exactly what pages they visit when they come to your website. A buyer coming from a landing page will browse your site differently when compared to someone who has actively searched for your website.

How Did the Buyer Get to Your Website?

Apart from being a business portal, your website serves many purposes - such as acting as an information portal, FAQ center, contact point, and marketing tool, all combined into one. As such, it's not enough for your website to just look professional.

Your website needs to be easily discoverable to all kinds of people. Not everyone stumbles upon your website in the same way. Depending on the needs and circumstances, users might find your website either by searching for you via a search engine (SEO), via social media or by coming across an online ad of yours.

In this section, I will explain how different buyers arrive at your website.

"Your website needs to be easily discoverable to all kinds of people. Not everyone stumbles upon your website in the same way."

Users who find your website via Search Engine (SEO) are the users who are searching or researching for a particular topic on Google. SEO is the process of generating traffic to your website by increasing the visibility of your website through search engines. Google and other search engines play a vital role in helping people find and research just about anything. So, when one person is trying to research their requirements, they will find your site information on Google, and then come to your website.

Let me explain this better with the help of an example. Let's imagine that a business owner is interested in developing a mobile app to further facilitate his business. He opens Google, which is the world's most popular search engine and enters the keywords "best mobile app development company" into the search bar. The results page then shows a bunch of results that it thinks are the best results, based on the query. He goes through the results and clicks on the one that he thinks is the best for him.

Images: Google Search Page

For these kinds of users, the chances of them ending up on your website greatly depends on how well the SEO of your site is done. This depends on both on-page and off-page SEO techniques. But content is also a major factor when it comes to SEO. We have all heard that "content is king", and that's a popular saying for a reason!

These users don't instantly end up on your website. It is a slow process, which involves extensive research.

We have seen that people need to find your website in Google results after typing some specific keywords. The quality of these keywords determines the chance of visitors converting to a lead.

Let me explain it a little more. Our website, royex.ae, ranks on Google's first page for several keywords – like, if you search "Mobile apps" or "Mobile apps development company Dubai", we'll appear. The first keywords there (Mobile apps) are very generic; the visitor may be looking for how to develop mobile apps, the best mobile apps, or anything else. With this keyword, it is tough to judge the visitor, and whether they are looking for a company to build its mobile app or not. On the other hand, the other keyword ("Mobile apps development company in Dubai") is very much specific; the visitor is looking for a company that can develop mobile apps and is based in Dubai. The chance of getting leads from this visitor is very, very high.

So it is important to find quality keywords for your website and rank those keywords on the first page of Google. Long-tail keywords always generate more leads.

"Long-tail keywords always generate more leads."

Keyword Research

At this point, you may want to know how to find the best keywords for your website, and what the process of finding the best keywords is. So, let me briefly explain keyword research.

It is the process of finding the words that people are using to search within search engines. It is done to optimize the content by strategically placing the keywords in your content, which will then help you to rank in search results for those keywords.

With keyword research, you can answer important questions like, "What exactly are people searching for?" and "How many people are searching for it?". By knowing what the users search and the quantity of those searches, you can create content that addresses the needs of those users.

Naturally, you would want to rank for keywords that most people use for searching, i.e. high-volume keywords, right? But how do you find these keywords? Let me take a moment to talk about the different ways I use to research keywords for preparing my website content.

I start with the main (or the seed) keywords that are going to be the foundation for my research. For example, as we know, I run a website and mobile app development company (Royex) based in Dubai. So my seed keywords are going to be something like:

Website design Dubai

Mobile app development Dubai

From here, I will develop keyword ideas that are relevant to the seed keywords. Using Google's Search Console, I can see what keywords I already rank for – and I will also find out what keywords my competitors are ranking for, and then try to rank for those keywords too.

Another method I use for finding keywords is using keyword research tools that give me an estimate of the number of people searching for that keyword so that I can learn which keywords to prioritize. Google AdWords Planner is great for this, as it gives you an estimate of the search volume of each keyword. Recently I started using neilpatel.com

Finally, I also use the features that are built into Google, such as auto-suggest and similar searches, to get more keyword ideas. I combine all the information at hand, listing all the keywords in an excel sheet, and produce content for them.

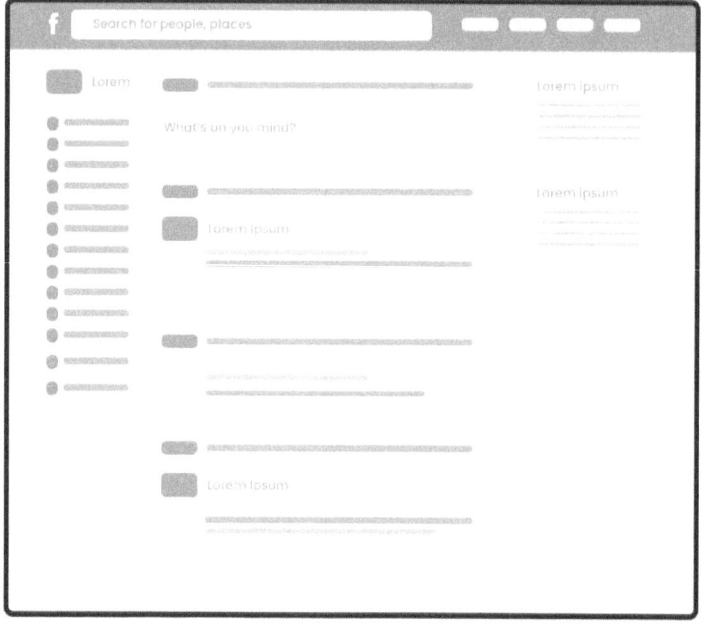

Image: Social Media

The traffic that originates from social media is simply referred to as social media traffic. This is when a person browsing social media stumbles upon your Tweet or Facebook post and clicks the links that redirect them to your website. This traffic can be either paid or organic. One of the truly great things about social media is that it is used by all different age groups and on a global basis. Due to its massive popularity, it serves as the second-most significant source of traffic.

This type of traffic ends up on your website as a direct result of your social media marketing efforts. It involves posting on social media with a catchy caption and a link to your website page. It may also involve using multimedia, such as images, gifs, and videos to attract audiences.

In essence, these users don't search for your website themselves; rather, it is your social media presence that pulls them towards your site. Unlike SEO, this process isn't slow, and there is no research involved by the users.

The probability of a user clicking on your link over social media depends on a few factors. First of all, the content you are marketing should be relevant to them. The caption you use should be catchy, as well. Oftentimes, users will simply click on a post because the caption or the image used was enough to grab their attention!

Businesses are now focusing more and more towards social media, and are treating it seriously in today's age. And of course, with the number of mobile users increasing exponentially, the impact of social media is only going to continue growing and will continue to serve as a major traffic source for websites.

Tips to generate traffic from Social Media

Here are some handy tips for generating traffic from social media:

o **Use attention-grabbing visuals:** In social media, grabbing the user's attention is quite a challenge, as they are always scrolling through. If you complement your post with an eye-appealing image, they might very well stop and see what you have to say.

o **Engage with your audience:** Social media platforms allow you to interact with your audience directly. Use this to your advantage and interact with them by commenting, replying to their messages, and listening to their needs.

o **Post regularly:** With hundreds of posts on social media, it is very easy for people to forget about a single brand. However, when you post regularly, users are constantly being reminded of you. There are optimal posting frequencies and times that you need to find out for your brand.

o **Create viral content:** If you create viral, unique content that your users love, they will share it - and ultimately, this will serve to drive a lot of traffic to your website. Content like short videos, memes, and infographics tends to go more viral than other types of content.

o **Include your URL in your posts:** Link your website in all of your social media posts, so that you can get users to click on them and visit your website. Social signals are also great for SEO, and it's great to improve the website's authority.

Landing Page

Another way users get to your website is by clicking on an ad that redirects them to a landing page on your website. They see the ad as a result of an ad campaign that you've run to generate more traffic to your website.

One popular ad campaign medium is Google AdWords, in which Google displays your ad for a particular keyword that you target. This ad then shows up when users query for that keyword. The ad contains a title and a link to a page - which is known as the landing page.

Other web pages have many purposes to fulfill, but landing pages have only one purpose: to get the user to either fill in their information via a contact form or to click on the CTA button to make a purchase.

Once the user lands on this page and enters this information, you have successfully acquired a lead. Landing pages also contain videos to supplement the content on that page. Videos present the information more interactively, making it easy for users to understand what you're offering.

You might additionally insert some relevant links on the landing page so that users can get to know more about you and your business.

Users don't need to find your landing page through the ad campaign necessarily. It is also possible that they came from one of your social media channels. Nowadays, it's common practice to advertise your landing page directly on social media sites for more opportunities. In a later chapter, we're going to touch on this a bit more and discuss designing landing pages.

Tips to generate traffic from Google AdWords

Here are some tips for generating traffic from Google AdWords:

- o **Increase your daily budget:** This might seem like an obvious one, but if you want more traffic from AdWords, you need to increase your budget to show more ads and get more clicks.
- o **Expand the location for your ads:** By expanding the geographic area of where your ads will be shown, you can increase the size of your audience and naturally gain more traffic.

o **Add more relevant keywords:** With a higher number of keywords, AdWords will match your ad to more search queries, and hence, you'll obtain more impressions and traffic.

o **Extend your ad schedule:** Run your ad schedule during times that are compatible with your business. Extending to weekends will increase the periods that your ads are shown, and will certainly result in more traffic.

o **Include search partners in your network:** This is an option you can enable in Google AdWords settings. Upon enabling this, your ad will show up on other sites, such as Google Maps, YouTube, etc.

Tips to generate traffic from Facebook Ads

Here are some tips for generating traffic from Facebook Ads:

o **Optimize your ad schedule:** There are always optimal times to run your ads when they'll get the most clicks. It's up to you to find the hours and the days that these ads will perform the best, and then schedule them out for those times.

o **Rotate your ads frequently:** Instead of posting the same ad over and over again, try rotating your ads frequently, and you could see an increase in the number of clicks you receive.

o **Optimize your ad placement:** You can check the top-performing ads on the Facebook Ads Manager and increase your bids on them. Remove the ads that are performing poorly.

o **Use A/B testing for ads:** A/B testing allows you to find out what works best for you. You can test your ad design, your offer, CTAs, and design, to find the most optimal ones.

o **Choose the right campaign objective:** You can choose this when creating a new ad campaign on Facebook. Among the objectives are awareness, consideration, and conversion. You need to choose the one which best suits your objective.

How Does The Buyer Navigate Your Website?

As we have seen, users get to your website through SEO, social media, or a landing page. How users navigate your website depends heavily upon how they found your website. Therefore, someone who came from a Google search will browse your site differently from someone who clicked on a landing page.

"Source of traffic dictates the visitor's navigational behavior. Build your site based on that."

Buyers coming from a Search Engine

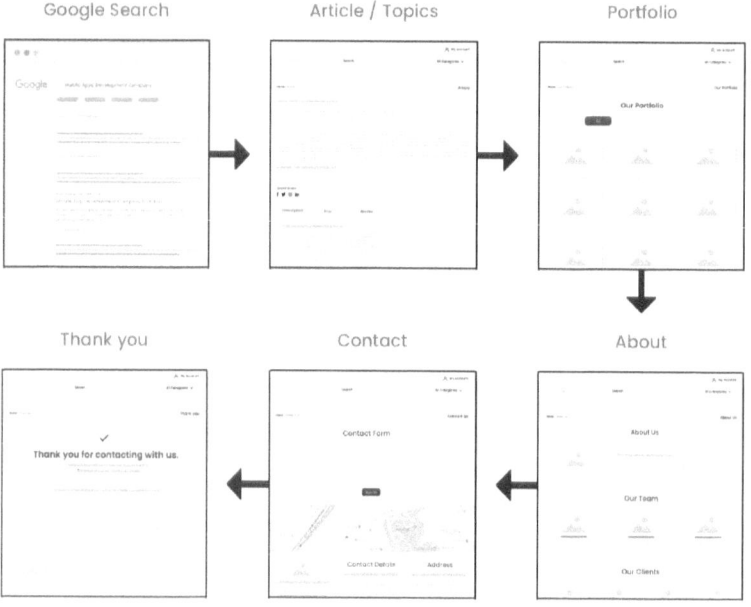

Images: Buyer's navigation when they come from search engines

Let's explain the buyer navigation here with the help of an example. Consider a user who searches the term "development cost of noon.com". After analyzing the Google search results, he decides to visit your website. Upon clicking the link, he is redirected to an article that you've written, covering the development cost of noon.com.

At the end of the article, the website development service page has been linked. The user then navigates to the service page, to learn about your web design services. He might be interested in your services, but he also needs to see some of your previous work to judge its quality.

Hence, from the services page, he will then navigate to the portfolio page and assess your past work. After he's done doing that, he wants to know more about your company and will move to the About Us page. At this stage, he has read your article, checked out your service page, glanced at your portfolio, and learned about your company.

Now he wants to contact you and discuss the services you can offer to him. He goes to the contact page and submits his information via the contact form. That redirects him to the Thank You page, where you express your gratitude for him contacting you, and then inform him that you will get back to him soon. This completes his navigation on the website.

The chances of lead generation are quite high when users come from search engines because they inquire about what you have to offer, and are thus interested in it.

Buyers Coming From Social Media Channels

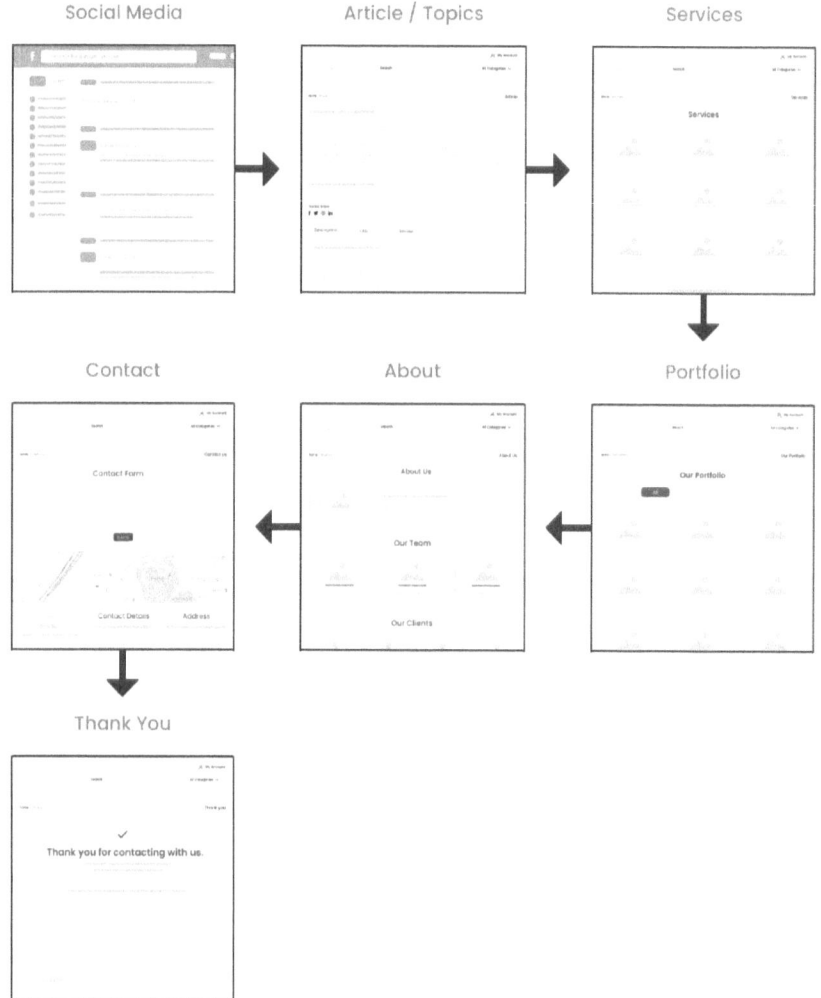

Image: Buyer navigation when they come from social media

Remember: someone who finds your website through a social media platform didn't search for you. He stumbled upon your post and was interested in learning more about what you had to offer. For example, let's say that he clicked on a post on your Facebook page titled "Best SEO practices to follow", which redirects to an article on your website that explains the topic.

So the first page he visits on your website is that article. In the article, you have linked to your SEO service page, for your visitors to see what kind of SEO services you offer. Once the visitor goes to your service page, he will then want to see some of your work as proof of service.

He will head to the portfolio page, where you have listed projects you have completed in the past. Now he knows about the services you offer, and what kind of projects you have dealt with! His next step will be to learn more about your company.

He will browse over to the About Us section of your website, reading up about your company – and if he is satisfied with what he has seen so far, he's going to want to contact you and get a quote on your SEO services. He goes to the contact page and submits his information via the contact form. That redirects him to the Thank You page, in which you express your gratitude for him contacting you, and inform him that you will get back to him soon. This completes his navigation on the website.

The chances of lead generation are quite low for users coming from social media when compared to that of search engines. These users haven't originally searched for anything in the first place, and it is your post that lured them to your website. The dropouts are quite high for these kinds of users, and all you can do is build your branding image for them, and expect that they will visit you in the future on their own.

Buyers Coming From a Landing Page

Image: Buyer navigation when they come from a landing page

These are users who came across an ad in search engines or social media. Either way, they don't go directly to your website, but instead, land on a custom-made page that has been designed with a particular goal and a CTA button. The goal may be to sell you a single product/service, or otherwise for lead generation.

As landing pages are designed to keep the user focused, unnecessary distractions, such as other forms of site navigation, are not present here. But most landing pages have the company on the upper top, allowing users to go to the homepage and find out more about them.

So in this case, the methods of buyer navigation can be varied. If the buyer is heavily impressed with the landing page, they may directly go for the purchase and proceed to the checkout page! But in other cases, more diligent buyers may opt to research more about the company first.

And then they follow the usual navigation of browsing the website and gathering as much information as possible, before finally deciding to commit. The better-designed the landing page, the better the chances of converting are.

At the end of the day, the goal of your business site is to make the sale, no matter where the buyer comes from. You will learn more about this in the upcoming chapters.

Now we know how a visitor is going to behave when they appear on your website. Is your website designed in such a way to facilitate your visitors? Find out what is lacking and start building upon those foundations. Later on, in Chapter 7, we will list all the elements you need to have on a specific page to attract visitors and convince them to generate leads.

Chapter 3

Reasons Websites Fail to Generate

Leads

If your website gets a lot of visitors but fails to generate leads, then there's something wrong that you need to address and fix immediately.

In this chapter, I'm going to go over these problems and categorize them into four categories, so that it's easier to understand.

Fixing these issues will not only get your website back on track to be a lead magnet, but will also increase its authority, trust, and traffic.

Trust Issue

Prospective clients are now doing more research and vetting than ever, and your website is a key determinant in helping them to decide if you're legit and can be trusted.

Here are 8 factors that can damage trust and hurt your credibility, when people are first visiting your website to check you out:

1. Your real contact information is missing: Simply listing your email address and social media isn't enough here. You need to have your physical address listed on your website in the Contact Us section. Real-world information goes a long way in building trust and authenticity. Be sure to also list your phone number, along with local area code, instead of a toll-free number. You could additionally opt to go the extra mile and show your physical address via online maps.

2. Poorly-designed About page: The majority of visitors to your website are going to want to know a bit about you before they begin doing business with you. The "About Us" section of your website exists for that very purpose and is one of the most visited pages of your entire website, period. The websites that fail to generate leads usually fill up this page with boring details that nobody wants to hear about. What you can do instead, is use this page to tell your story, and give the users a chance to get to know you better and on a more personal level.

3. Lack of testimonials: One of the best ways to prove your credibility is to showcase reviews from real people. People demand to see these before they purchase your goods/services. A trusted website will show what other clients have been saying about them. It serves as proof of your excellent service, and of the fact that people can trust you. Testimonials from real people, along with their photographs and names, is something you absolutely must include in your website, if you want to gain trust and credibility.

4. Lack of case studies: Case studies are a great way to show how your service has helped people and benefited them. For example, if you run a website that offers online coaching for weight loss, it would be really helpful if you provided case studies of your existing clients (with their permission, of course). These case studies can show the before and after pics of your clients' weight loss transformation after availing your service. New prospective clients will trust you and your services then, once they see these studies, and will want to avail of your service.

5. Not stating the obvious: There are many obvious questions that prospective clients have in their mind when they visit your website. You need to address them by having this information clearly stated on your website:

- o **Cost:** This is the most obvious of all questions that clients are going to have. If your price matches their budget, only then will they start to look into all the other details. Whether it is a service or a product you're selling, you need to mention your cost, including all charges. If you are offering custom solutions, then at least give an estimate of the costs and list out the variables involved in the cost. If you offer high-end products, you might think listing your price will drive people away - but that is not the case. The ones who can afford your product will value it, and the ones that can't afford it won't waste their time (or yours).

o **Pros and cons:** One major mistake businesses make is not being completely genuine when they talk about their products and services. They only write about the positives and completely avoid mentioning any of its cons. But we all know that no product or service is the perfect fit for all, and it is far better for you to be honest and be transparent in this regard. This way, you will earn respect and trust from your clients.

o **Competitors and other solutions:** Another way of building trust among your users is to acknowledge the existing competition and alternate solutions. There will always be someone out there who is offering cheaper prices than you, and that's okay. In this case, you could talk about how your products have better quality and craftsmanship than the competition. This builds more trust and encourages openness with your clients.

6. No incentives: One of the best lead generation methods is to offer free samples and trials to the visitors of your website. If you offer something valuable to them, they will acknowledge the incentive - and if they like your free sample/trial, they will go for the purchase! It is a great way of building interest and generating sales.

7. Unappealing website design: If your website just does not look good, then visitors won't even bother checking out what you have to offer. This significantly reduces your chances of them converting them into leads. I'm going to talk about website design in great detail later on.

Traffic Issue

The best website in the world isn't going to generate leads without traffic. Not only do you need a sufficient volume of traffic to your site - but you also need the right type of traffic.

1. **Insufficient traffic:** There is a direct correlation between traffic and leads. The quantity of leads generated depends on how well your website is doing, in terms of traffic. Let's say we have a target of 200 leads per month. To achieve that, let's say you need at least 2000 unique visitors to your website. But if you are getting only 500 visitors per month, then your priority would be to fix the traffic issue, first and foremost.

   To do this, you need to focus on these three sources of traffic:

   o **Paid advertising:** If you have some money to work with, you can start driving visitors to your site within mere hours! Facebook and Google are where the action is, and they can supply you with all the traffic you'll ever need. But be careful, because you can run up a pretty huge tab in a hurry if you don't know what you're doing.

   o **SEO:** I discussed SEO in the previous chapter, which is essentially the actions you perform to increase the search engine rankings of your webpages. So when someone searches for a topic that your website has content on, it will appear higher in the search results, and thus resulting in increased traffic.

o **Free Tools:** You can offer free incentives, such as ebooks, tools, reports, etc. to help drive more traffic toward your website. These are great for both lead generation and traffic generation. And if you make it a regular thing, you will also find visitors returning so that they can access the free content.

"The best website in the world isn't going to generate leads without traffic"

2. **Wrong traffic:** It doesn't matter if you have a lot of traffic to your website if they're not the right kind of traffic. What you want is for this traffic to convert into leads – and they will only do so if they are interested in what you have to offer. One correct way of attracting the right traffic is to write articles addressing their needs and concerns.

For example, if your website offers domain and hosting solutions, but offers content on Artificial Intelligence, then there is going to be a conflict of interest there. You very well may generate a lot of traffic by writing content on AI, as it's a very trendy and popular topic at the moment, but that kind of traffic is wrong for your website because they're not going to be interested in your domain and hosting solutions. Not all traffic is the same.

Lead Mechanics Issue

o **Unclear message:** Consumers don't like being confused, and they shouldn't feel confused when they visit your website. If your website doesn't convey the message loud and clear, then they might leave and just go somewhere else. Take your time to craft a well-written message that clearly defines and states what your users are looking for.

o **Not using bullets points:** Bullet points are great for a lot of reasons. Nobody wants to read a huge block of text and waste their time searching for information. They expect websites to list key info in bullet points so that they can concisely get the information. Bullet points are short sentences that state only the important message, and you can use this format to easily describe your services or the benefits your business offers.

o **Not reminding them of their issues:** The demand for a product or a service arises from an issue or a challenge that a customer is facing. And this is precisely why they visit your website to look for a solution to their problem. Your task is to remind them of their problem and pain, to force them to take action. This must be done in a way that doesn't offend them, while at the same time building an emotional connection with them because you have addressed their issues and are offering to provide a solution.

o **Failure to create urgency:** Your website must build a sense of urgency, to force the user to take an initiative. The best way to do this is by offering a limited time discount or offer that is simply too good to refuse. You can also pair this up with any occasion (such as New Years, for example), to make it more lucrative.

o **Not convincing users:** Many website owners make the mistake of not asking their users to buy their products and services. Honestly, this might seem pushy and counterproductive, but by just asking them to buy from you (without being over the top), this can work really well for you. You can use popups, sliders, and footers to remind them to make a purchase.

o **Not offering value:** Many businesses fail to give users a single reason to ever return to their website. This is an extremely important area to look at because the majority of potential customers are not going to purchase something from you on their first visit. The first visit is usually focused on getting to know you and your business – and as a result, they tend to forget about you once they have left your website, and now you have lost them forever. So, to counteract this, you need to offer them something before they leave. For example, you could offer them a free ebook, or a report, in exchange for their email address.

Now you have got yourself a leader, whom you can contact further down the line!

○ **No experimenting or testing:** Many websites are afraid of experimenting with their website features and design, opting instead for a "safe" option and leaving it as it is. The truth is, you need to keep experimenting with the features of your websites, such as the layout, design, images, etc., to see how users respond. After all, their response is what matters, and you must provide them with the best possible experience, to ensure maximum lead generation.

○ **Not tracking statistics:** A free tracking tool like Google Analytics goes a long way in helping you analyze your website's performance. Instead of guessing and estimating, tracking software or tool will tell you exactly what's working and what isn't. You can then use this information to make changes to your website and enhance its performance, ultimately leading to more lead generation.

Other Issues

Your website is generic

Nowadays, it has become easier than ever to design websites, thanks to website builders that make the whole process straightforward and easy. But the issue is, almost all the websites that are built this way inevitably end up looking the same, more or less. There is nothing unique about the website built with these sites. This will draw your users away. You need custom-designed websites that stand out, both in terms of look and feel.

Lack of human touch on your website

If your website visitors feel that your website feels too robotic, or formal, they will quickly lose touch with it. You need them to feel as if they are interacting with real people, instead of with a machine. Your "About Us" page can add a personal touch by sharing your company story, adding images of your employees, and helping users connect with you.

You can add images of you, your employees, and your office, to inject a true sense of realism into your website.

For instance, our website, royex.ae always uses real images that represent and express our company. But if we had just used boring, stock images, you might consider us a generic company with no human touch. Since we use the images of our team, though, you feel connected and confident when you meet us.

Lack of funnel structure in your website

You aim to design your website in such a way that it functions as a conversion funnel. Right from the moment someone reaches the homepage, you should be leading your users to a landing page with a clear CTA that will ultimately lead to a conversion.

Chapter 4

Learn Before Designing Your

Website

As I mentioned before, this book is not just about some tips to make your website look good. My goal here is to make you knowledgeable on different things that will all help you to fully understand the lead generation process. This is one of the very important chapters of this book, in which you will come to understand several things.

In this chapter, you will learn about concepts such as SEO, Digital Marketing, Landing pages, and UI/UX, which are very crucial to website development and design. You cannot design a lead generating website without implementing these concepts on your site.

The website design process is different from person to person, and industry to industry. A website that provides mobile app development, naturally, will have a different approach to website design when compared to a website that offers interior design services. By the end of this chapter, you will learn what to keep in mind, before you implement your website design.

Search Engine Optimization (SEO)

What SEO Is, and How It Works

SEO is a process that generates traffic to your website by changing the content in a way that makes it visible on common search engine results.

You adjust the content and layout of your website page in such a way that it is more attractive to all common search engines and, in effect, shows up in the search results. Sometimes it can all seem quite complicated, but the basic technique of SEO is not hard to understand.

Various search engines compete to provide the best services for their users. They scan through various websites and assess their content thoroughly, finding the websites that fulfill their criteria, to provide the most optimal results for their users that are of the top-most quality. They do this through relevant topics or keywords. At the same time, search engines also calculate website speed, in addition to assessing how easy to use and understand it is for all users. Only those websites meeting all the criteria set by search engines show up on the top of their results.

Organizations employ SEO techniques to ensure that their websites are the most visible in search results. They also use words and phrases that are of the most relevance, which are then detected by search engine algorithms. For example, if you wanted to publish an article on how to develop a website, you would use relevant phrases, wording your blog in such a way that it shows up on the top results, whenever someone searches the phrase "develop a website" online.

SEO is very beneficial for your company, and you can bring in many potential customers by employing effective SEO techniques. This can increase your chances of effective business contact.

Factors That Impact SEO

Several factors have an impact on search engine rankings. Although Google does not reveal its exact algorithms, we can still understand some of the factors that have a direct impact on search engine results. Some are on-page, while some are off-page. These are discussed below.

Content Marketing

"Content Marketing is all the Marketing that's left."

~ Seth Godin

The written and image content that you show on your website is one of the top-most and important factors for your company. It should be of the highest quality so that it gets the top-most ranking from search engines. Furthermore, this is also the basis to engage your users and retain them on the page, fully maximizing your chances of making sales.

One of the most effective ways of ensuring that the impact of your website content is effectively maximized is to have a variety of content covering a wide range of topics, to ensure the greatest chances of it matching up with users' search results. Some types of content could be:

- o Blog posts and articles
- o Social media content
- o Ebooks and white papers
- o How-To Guides and Tutorials
- o Videos and audio recordings
- o Infographics or other visual content

Another important tip for SEO is to use certain words and phrases that users are most likely to type in when searching for their required content. These words should be reflective of your business, but also common enough that there is a high chance that people use them while searching for your product or service online. This increases your chances of getting a good search engine ranking.

A crucial aspect of having good content on your website is freshness, which essentially refers to how often the website is updated with new content. This does not only include uploading new articles, or blogs, etc., but also encompasses updating any previous content so that it can keep users engaged for longer periods.

Although content creation requires time and resources, it is an important investment to obtain good potential customers through your website, and eventually pays out in the form of successful business from these users. It also helps in gaining a following on social media, which can then be used to access an even wider range of potential customers.

On-Page SEO

As suggested by the name, the on-page SEO factors are those that influence your webpage directly. They are completely under your control, and you need to focus on them to improve your website ranking. This not only involves marketing your content but also includes several other factors from your website's HTML. Some of these factors are:

Title Tag – The phrase on each page that tells the search engine about your page, including the company name and the keywords that your page focuses on. Your title tag should not exceed 60 characters in length.

Meta Description – This gives some more details about your page to the search engines, as well as to the page visitors. It should include main keywords so that users find it relevant, and engage more readers that are your potential customers.

Sub-headings – Including sub-headings in your content makes it easier for users to skim through your website, while concurrently making it more attractive. This is an important aspect of good SEO. The H1, H2 and H3 tags enable search engines to understand these subheadings better.

Internal Links – Several pages on your website can be interlinked through internal links or hyperlinks. These allow search engines to scroll through your website, and also help users to find out more information that they require. For example, in a blog about a product or service you offer, you can include a hyperlink to the product page on your website, for the users' ease of reference.

Image Name and ALT Tags – Using the alt tag, or keywords for image names and description increases the chances of the image showing up in search engine results. It will also enable search engines to understand your webpage better and improve your ranking.

When using SEO keywords and phrases in your website content, it is also important not to overdo it, as that will hurt your search engine ranking. Furthermore, you should also be careful about creating focused content that deals with just the most relevant keywords. You should use only specific content. Using too many keywords or random phrases that cover a broader range of topics just depicts unfocused, thin content, which adds up to portray a bad image.

Although the content of your website is extremely important, the layout and site architecture also plays an equally key role in search engine rankings. The design should be easy to use and scroll through, both for the search engine and for the website visitors.

Creating interlinks between your website pages, building a proper sitemap, and submitting your website design to search engines can greatly improve the visibility of your website for these search engines.

Another crucial factor to consider is that your website design should be mobile-friendly. Many people these days are using mobile devices, rather than desktops, to surf the internet. Your website should allow these users to navigate through your page and to use it with ease. Allowing for this will not only impress users but will also improve your SEO and search engine rankings even further.

Off-Page SEO

Apart from on-page factors, there are also off-page SEO factors that are not directly in your control, but that you can tweak to your advantage. These have a direct impact on your ranking. Here are some of the off-page factors that build up your SEO rankings:

Trust – Users always prefer websites that have a good trust ranking with Google. Search engines determine the quality of trust by the number of backlinks your website has with good, legitimate websites. Therefore, if you want to improve your trust rankings with search engines, you should work on creating backlinks with pages that already have a very good trust in the market.

Links – a very common SEO tip is to create good backlinks on your websites. However, you should be careful about not overdoing it, as an excess of backlinks can be penalized by Google. You should work on building good relationships with companies, influencers, and customers who will allow you to create trusted backlinks to their pages, and thus help you improve your ranking.

Social – The content on your website should be of high quality, and make its presence felt on social media. Your popularity will earn you likes, shares, and follows, and in turn, will help you improve your visibility on search engines.

Although you cannot always directly control the off-page factors, you can work towards creating beautiful, high-quality content that will automatically improve your SEO ranking and your online visibility. If your content is more relevant and interesting for users, it only increases the chances of the users sharing it on social media. This works to improve trust for search engines, as they assess high traffic and sharing as being positive factors for good ranking.

Black Hat vs. White Hat SEO

There are two types of SEO tactics that companies can employ to improve their rankings. These are classified as "Black Hat" and "White Hat" SEO.

Black Hat SEO involves methods that only work in the short term to improve search engine rankings. These organizations focus on getting a good ranking in the short term and making money off of it, without making any long-term plans.

They do not focus on real human presence or sales; rather, they just go around loopholes and improve their rankings for the short term. They do not optimize their content for humans and focus only on search engines.

However, this approach results in websites that are not at all user-friendly, and the public does not like to visit these pages. They end up looking like spam sites. And although these show up high in rankings very quickly, they are also penalized and shut off very quickly. This is why these techniques work only in the short term.

In short, these get-rich-quick schemes only give short-term benefits, but end up ruining any chance for long-term, established business through your website pages.

In contrast, White Hat SEO is an approach that builds long term strategies to develop your website, generate good traffic, and sustain those visitors as regular customers. These tactics target real, human traffic, rather than merely getting a good ranking on search engines.

This type of SEO focuses on good quality content on your website that is user-friendly, easy to follow, and simple to understand. At the same time, they also abide by the rules and regulations set up by search engines.

You must understand that, although Black Hat SEO works quickly, it is doesn't work in the long term. Search engine algorithms eventually recognize them and are very likely to penalize them in turn. For more severe offenses, these penalties may even be permanent.

Therefore, you should focus on White Hat SEO, if you want to establish a strong foothold for your business and build a good relationship with customers. This will increase the presence of your webpage, as well as provide good, organic traffic. You should create the content of the highest quality and focus on visitors, rather than employing unprofessional tactics for search engine rankings.

Digital Marketing

What is Digital Marketing?

Digital marketing is the process of marketing your business online via electronic devices and the internet. Businesses utilize various online channels, such as search engines, social media, email, and other websites, to reach out to both prospective and external customers. In simple terms, any marketing that you perform over the internet is labeled as "digital marketing".

Traditional marketing used to be conducted through print ads, telephones, television, or direct physical marketing, whereas digital marketing takes place only electronically. This means that you can use your website, social media, email, video, etc. for your online marketing and branding efforts.

> *"Any marketing that you perform over the internet is labeled as digital marketing"*

In this day and age, digital marketing is crucial for your brand awareness and promotion. If you notice, most brands have a well-designed website, a highly active and interactive social media, and a solid digital marketing strategy all in place – and strong emphasis is placed on the website's content, as people depend on it to know more about the brands.

To turn your website into a lead machine, there is no alternative to digital marketing. Hence, in this section, I'm going to focus on digital marketing and what it can do for your brand.

Benefits of Digital Marketing

Many businesses have already experienced the advantages of digital marketing over traditional marketing means. Regardless of what your company sells, digital marketing can work effectively for any industry. With digital marketing, you can see results much faster than you might with old-fashioned offline marketing. Here are some of the benefits digital marketing has to offer:

Cost-effective: One of the largest benefits of online marketing is that it is cost-effective. Compared to traditional marketing, digital marketing can save you money, obtaining more leads in the process. You can optimize your website, add meaningful and shareable content, and utilize your social media to promote your brand, all without any extra investment.

Measurable: When you run a marketing campaign, you want to know how well it's performing. In digital marketing, everything is measurable. There are tracking systems that enable you to effectively measure and track your marketing campaigns.

Target the right customers: Reaching out to the wrong people will not give you anything. You need to spend your time and resources on targeting those who require your services. Fortunately, digital marketing allows you to do exactly that.

Dynamic: Another major advantage of digital marketing is that you can make changes on the go, to truly make the most out of your marketing campaign. Traditional marketing is limited to what you began with and making it work, but digital marketing is very flexible and dynamic.

Improved conversion rate: As digital marketing allows you to target your users to acquire leads, your conversion rates improve vastly. The whole campaign is centered around targeting those who are interested in your products and services.

Components of Digital Marketing

Digital Marketing is not just limited to one arena. It is a combination of several elements that all work together to form your marketing strategy. Here's a breakdown of the components of digital marketing:

Search Engine Optimization (SEO): I discussed SEO in the previous chapter. It is a component of digital marketing, because SEO improves the ranking of your website, along with its visibility in search engine results.

Almost 90% of people don't venture beyond the first page of search engine results. So naturally, your web page must rank on the first page! Through on-page and off-page SEO, you can optimize your website to increase its visibility. This will ultimately improve your leads.

Content marketing: Your website content helps your site rank higher, and also provides information to the prospective customers who are interested in learning more about your business. Content marketing is an excellent way to earn more leads and revenue.

The better the quality of your content, the better your rankings will be. Through quality content, you can target keywords related to user needs and your business. Make sure your content answers the questions your users are looking for. I will discuss website content in great detail in the next chapter.

Pay-per-click (PPC) advertising: Pay-per-click advertising is a great way to appear in search engine results, as you work your way through organic rankings through SEO, and it is one of the best ways to gather leads for your website.

Even though PPC is a paid form of digital marketing, it works wonderfully, because you only pay for the ads when people click on them. And those people click them because they are interested in your products and services - so you are getting quality leads while also avoiding wasting valuable time and money in pursuing people who have no interest in you.

You can target your ad campaign to people based on their age, gender, and demographics.

Social media marketing: Social media is a great platform to connect and interact with your existing and potential customers. It is used by the majority of people and serves as a free tool for developing a deeper connection with your customers.

It also allows you to know what consumers are talking about, and you can then use this information to cater to their needs. You can also run paid ads on social media targets to reach your preferred customers.

Social media can also be used for customer service and providing swift responses. In summary, it is a great element of digital marketing that can grow your business and promote your brand, as long as it's done correctly.

"Content is fire. Social media is gasoline."

~ Jay Baer

Email marketing: Email marketing is fantastic for generating leads, and is one of the most effective tools of digital marketing. For every $1 you invest in email marketing, you get a return of $44, returning a 4400% ROI.

Emails are great because users opt-in to receive your emails, making them targeted and potential customers. They express interest in your products and services and can be nurtured to become leads with emails that highlight your products/services. With automation tools, you can send thousands of emails with only a click, once again saving you valuable time and effort.

Video marketing: Videos have slowly toppled other forms of content, and are fast becoming many users' preferred form of content. As such, utilizing them in your digital marketing strategy is a surefire way of increasing your leads.

Short, well-made videos with animation and voiceover will generate a lot of traffic, compared to traditional images or text. Popular platforms like YouTube or Vimeo are great avenues to market your content, as these platforms have millions of users, and you get a lot of exposure.

Landing Page

What is a Landing Page?

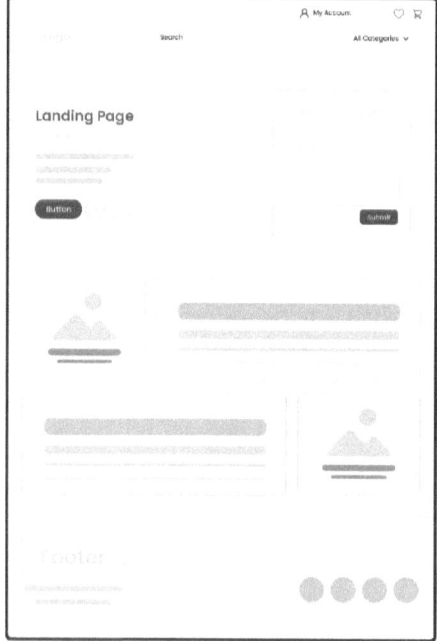

Image: Sample Landing Page

A landing page is a special area on your website that is designed with a specific purpose: converting visitors into leads. This page is different from other pages on your websites. They are not available on the sitemap itself and only appear on the ads of a marketing campaign.

A landing page has a form which collects the visitor's information, in exchange for an offer. In other cases, it might contain a selling speech, along with a CTA button, to get the visitor to make a purchase.

Landing pages are far more successful in acquiring a lead or making a purchase.

This is what happens when a visitor comes across a landing page:

- o They see an ad on the internet and click on it.
- o They are redirected to the landing page.
- o The page offers to give them something in return when they fill out a form.
- o The user fills out the form and becomes a lead.
- o You now have the information to contact the lead and market your product/service.

What You Need Before Creating a Landing Page

Before you learn how to design a landing page, you also need to know some things about your target buyers, to make sure that you are well-researched and informed about them:

The Buyer Persona(s)

I discussed buyer personas in an earlier chapter. These are detailed representations of your target customers that are formed after surveying and researching the market and customer data. They allow you to understand customer behavior and needs, as well as what (and how) they think.

So why is it important to form a buyer persona before you design your landing page? Well, by knowing about the customer and their needs, you can then work to create content that is specifically tailored to them. Every element on the landing page will target the persona, and that massively increases your chances of conversion.

The Offer

When you design a landing page, there's a contact form where the visitors can enter their contact information. You need to offer them some incentive to do so or get them to feel that they are valued. This can be in the form of an ebook, a report, a guide, a sheet, etc. that is useful to them. This incentive is called "the offer", and it should match with the issue that your buyer persona is going through.

The Buyer's Journey

The buyer's journey is the research process that a prospective buyer undergoes before making a purchase. It is a three-stage process, covering: awareness, consideration, and the decision stage. The content and the landing page elements must match with the corresponding stage of the buyer's journey that they are currently going through.

Landing Page Best Practices

Now that you've completed your research on the buyer, it is time to design your landing page! There are certain landing page design practices that you must follow, to maximize your conversions:

Write a catchy headline: You want a headline that catches the attention of your visitor quickly, and that makes them want to read what you have to offer. But at the same time, don't make outlandish claims that make your product/service seem too good to be true, or else they'll leave.

State your offer: The attention span of the average reader is quite low. This means you need to state what you have to offer before they lose interest. You need to describe your offer concisely and simply.

Include bullet points: To continue off of the last point, when information is presented in a lengthy paragraph, it becomes difficult to skim through the key points. This may result in the visitor missing your offer. Bullet points, however, are great for presenting the information in an organized, clear manner. They keep the reader interested and ultimately increase the chances of them converting.

Contact form: The form that you create must correspond with the buyer's journey state so that they can relate to it. Some basic information is always common in a form - such as a name and an email address. But as the lead advances further towards buying, you should add more fields to the form. Once they have reached the decision stage, you'll want as much information as possible, so that you can assist them better and close the sale.

Leave out site navigation: On any other page of your site, site navigation is an absolute must, so that the visitor will be able to browse around your website and get to know as much as they possibly can. But on a landing page, it is better to leave it out, as you want them to focus on the content and offers, instead of getting distracted and going to some other page.

Add images and videos: Relevant images and videos go a long way in grabbing the user's attention and making them stay on the site. A video or infographic can also supplement your content and help the user understand everything better. You can condense a lot of information down into an image or a video, and it's also far more interactive than simply having a wall of text.

Add user testimonials: No matter how appealing your offer may seem to the visitor, they still may seem skeptical of your product/service. Testimonials are a great way to instill a sense of trust and confidence in them, however, and can be of great help in convincing them. The testimonials on your website should also feature the name and image of the user, to add even more credibility and genuineness.

Clear instructions: When the visitor sees a form, it is implied that they will fill it out. However, it is still better for you to include an instruction that states something like, "Fill out the form below to access the ebook." This tells your visitor exactly what they need to do, and improves the chances of conversions.

UI and UX

User interface (UI) is a series of screens, pages, and design elements that allow a person to interact with a software or hardware device.

User experience (UX) is the experience a person has when they interact with a software or hardware device.

People often get confused between the two, thinking that they're similar concepts, but in reality, they're quite different from one another. In this section, I will explain the two in detail, as well as highlight their difference.

What is UI?

As explained above, a User Interface (UI) comprises anything that a user interacts with to access and use a product or service. This can include input devices like keyboards and mice, or visual media, such as screens.

The everyday devices that we use, such as our computers, smartphones, tablets, etc. all have user interfaces that allow us to interact with them. For example, in the case of a smartphone, this would be the touchscreen and the physical buttons that all help us use the device. When it comes to browsing a website, the buttons and navigation tools you use are the user interface elements of that website.

The difference between good and bad UI design is the level of usability and intuitiveness. Good UI design can be achieved by learning user behavior, pattern, biases, behavior, intuition, and perception. When done right, a good UI allows the user to effortlessly use the product or service, without needing any instructions or running into any issues.

Apart from the design element, UI also comprises the look, feel aesthetics, interactiveness, and responsiveness of a website – all of which combine to present a final interactive experience to the user.

Why is UI design important?

Consider the following situation: If you visited a website and couldn't navigate their website, what are the chances that you would leave that site and just go to another one? I'm willing to bet they're pretty high! Because of their poor user interface design, you're going to exit that site in a hurry.

If you run your business via a website, then, you must make that website easy and intuitive to use. A website's UI can be directly correlated to the traffic it receives. It is the reason why users are going to visit your website and want to stay there.

The tiniest improvements in UI can exponentially improve your website, and this is exactly why you cannot overlook this part of your business. These improvements will enhance your conversion rates vastly, and that means that your sales and customers are also going to increase. On the flip side, bad user experience can be horrible for your business, and can easily damage your reputation.

The main challenge here is that user interface design is not a one-time thing that you can just do once and then forget about it forever; user preference is an ongoing, evolving thing, and you must evolve along with it. Being dynamic and responding to their needs will put you ahead of the competition.

What is UX?

User experience, or UX, is the experience of users that results from their interaction with a product or a service. UX design works to take all the elements that are responsible for the experience into consideration, along with how the users perceive and interact with it.

Cognitive scientist Don Norman coined with the term "user experience" in the early '90s, and gave the following definition for it: User experience encompasses all aspects of the end-users interaction with the company, its services, and its products.

UX aims to create easy, intuitive, relevant, and meaningful experiences for the users when interacting with the product or the service.

Peter Morville developed the facets of UX design - known as the usability honeycomb. This honeycomb is used as a base guide for UX designers all over the world to understand effective design. It helps them to answer the following questions:

- o How the users would find your company's product or service
- o How they would interact with the interface of the product/service
- o How they would feel when trying to perform their task
- o What impressions they would form from the interaction experience

Why is UX design important?

Like UI, UX is also an important element in forming a positive experience, and understanding and meeting user needs. A good UX design will be able to enhance and ease the user's experience when interacting with your product/service. The user will want to use your product/service to save time, effort, and money.

But what matters more, is how happy or positive the user feels. Improving their experience is the ultimate end goal of UX design. Users have a positive experience when the UX is:

o Dependable

o Conversational

o Encouraging

o Personable

o Utilitarian

o Shareable

Without a good UX design, the user finds no value or incentive in using your product or service, and would instantly switch to other alternatives, once presented with them. UX is responsible for providing functionality to make the whole experience easier and beneficial for the user.

If you want to improve your relationship with the user and increase their satisfaction, improving your UX should be your top priority.

"If you do build a great experience, customers tell each other about that. Word of mouth is very powerful."

— Jeff Bezos

UI vs. UX: Two different concepts that work together

UI and UX design might be two different concepts, but at the same time, they are interconnected with one another. The common bond that exists between them is that they're both focused on ensuring maximum user satisfaction, they both depend upon each other's success, and one cannot shine without the other.

You cannot have a good-looking design with an interface that's bothersome and unintuitive to use; and similarly, well-designed user experience cannot afford to have a generic-looking, uninspiring visual design! Hence, both must work in tandem with one another to create the best user interaction possible.

The UI designer understands what needs to be done to create a good-looking user interface, and a UX designer makes the user interface intuitive and pleasant to use. This is a joint effort, which requires the two design teams to work together, to ultimately succeed.

The UX designer decides on how the elements work and navigate, and the UI designer decides how these interface elements will be displayed.

If at some stage in the design process, there's a need for extra elements to be added, the UX team will then change the layout of the elements, while the UI will modify the design to adjust to the new layout.

Hence, cooperation and collaboration between the UI and UX team are immensely important, in ensuring that the result, i.e. the final user interface, looks great and operates efficiently.

How to improve UI and UX to get more conversions

I've already discussed the benefits of UI and UX design, and how they can ultimately lead to more conversions - but how exactly can you improve the UI and UX of your website? In this section, you're going to learn how to do so!

Keep CTAs separate

Many websites make the mistake of pairing multiple CTAs next to each other to save space, or just to go for a consistent design. This is a big mistake. If you have multiple CTAs, don't put them on top or next to each other.

If you do, you will reduce the clicks that both CTAs get, and you also run the risk of confusing the user. You can test this out by running a heat map of your website. Adjacent CTAs don't get the attention that individuals CTAs get, and it defeats their whole purpose.

The best practice would be to keep them separate from one another. If you add one in the middle of a post, you can add another at the bottom, so that both get enough attention. It also serves as a constant reminder of your offer, as the user scrolls through your post.

Understand user behavior

If you want to improve conversions, you need to have a great UI and UX - we've already established that. But *how* do you do that? Easy: by understanding user behavior! In the context of a website, this relates to what a user does when they visit your website.

You can use this information to improve any weaknesses and optimize your website for future visitors. An easy way of understanding user behavior is through a scroll map, which displays your website through different colors, where each color indicates the time spent.

Red usually indicates the areas where the users spend most of their time, with blue indicating areas that are less looked-upon, and with green lying between red and blue. This data can be used to improve the layout of your website, and getting users to stay on the site more.

Optimize important pages first

Let's face it: not all the pages on your website are equally important. Some have more priority than others, and you need to shift your focus to these pages first. Your homepage, landing pages, product/service pages, and contact us page are some of the areas that need to be optimized first.

However, the actual priority of each page can depend, from business to business. For an e-commerce website, for instance, improving the products page would likely be their best bet. But the key here is to focus on one page, instead of trying to do them all together at once. Run some A/B tests, analyze the page performance, and then make other optimizations before moving on to the next page.

Decrease distractions on the sales page

One barrier to getting visitors to convert is distracting the users with excessive navigational links on your sales and landing pages. These pages are designed to convert, and so you don't need to have any extra links here that serve no purpose.

Decluttering these links from the page can make it easier for the user to focus on what you have to offer, and increase your conversion rate. On any other page of the website, you can add these links to make it easier for the user to traverse the website.

Keep the checkout simple

Generally, it is a good idea to make your website aesthetically pleasing, featuring attractive icons, images, videos. These can make your site look good and attract visitors. But when it comes to the checkout section of your website, keeping it simple should be the goal.

This is the section where the user has decided to make a purchase - and therefore, there should be no distractions present to drive them away. All those fancy graphics you put into the site were meant to make the user stay and convert. Now that they've decided to do so, you no longer need to have them there.

Only key information that pertains to the checkout information should be present on this page. Here at this final stage of making the purchase, you don't want to risk the sale of a product or service by adding something irrelevant or unnecessary onto the page!

Error-friendly messages

When visitors browse through your website, they expect easy, convenient navigation. However, it is common for visitors to face issues when browsing a website, which could be due either to a lack of understanding on their part or to some fault on your website.

Either way, you should display error messages for such issues. This way, they'll know what went wrong, and they won't panic. But of course, just showing a generic error message like "an error has occurred" won't help the user at all, and they might end up leaving your site. Conversely, a simple message explaining what went wrong goes a long way in reassuring the users.

The user must feel like they're talking to a person, and not just some computer code. A friendly error message is a great way to inform the user about the issue, and at the same time develop a connection with them.

Chapter 5

Website Content

High-quality content is vital to the success of any website, in gaining traffic and conversions. But what exactly do we mean by "high-quality content"? Can you just write any content and expect users to read and share it?

You've heard the phrase "content is king", and that's a popular saying for a very good reason! Good content is ranked high in search engines, shared by users on social media, adds value to your product/service, drives traffic to your site, and most importantly... generates leads and sales for your website.

"Great marketing is all about telling your story in such a way that it compels people to buy what you are selling."

~ Gary Vaynerchuck

In this chapter, I will teach you exactly how to write high ranking content for your website by dividing the content based on the buyer's journey.

What is Website Content?

Web content refers to the textual, aural, or visual content published on a website. Content can be defined by any creative element therein – such as, for example, text, applications, images, archived email messages, data, e-services, audio/video files, and so on.

There are two basic kinds of web content:

Text: Text is simple. It is added onto the web page as text blocks or within images. The best-written content is unique, textual web content that is free from plagiarism. Web content added as text can also include good internal links which help readers to gain access to more information.

Multimedia: Another kind of web content is multimedia. Simply put, multimedia refers to any content which is not text. Some examples include:

- o **Animations**: Animations can be added with the help of Flash, Ajax, and GIF images, as well as other animation tools.

o **Images**: Images are oft-considered the most popular option for incorporating multimedia into websites. Clip art, photos, or even drawings can be created using a scanner or a graphics editor. It is further recommended that you optimize the images so that your users can access and download them quickly.

o **Audio:** Different types of audio files can be added as part of the web content, to increase the website's desirability.

o **Video:** Video is also a wildly popular form of multimedia content; however, when adding video files, the publishers should also make sure that they work efficiently across various browsers.

Why is content important to generate leads for a website?

To run your website successfully, you need to have some web content management in place, which will allow you to plan and organize your content, concerning the needs of your readers.

Content plays a tremendous role in your website; it is the very reason why visitors come to you. Content takes priority over your design, site architecture, CMS, etc. Don't get me wrong, these are all important for your website too - but for the user, the content is much more important. Quality content will ensure that your content is shared, saved, and referred; whereas poorly-written content will serve only to drive visitors away.

Aesthetics and design alone won't simply help you rank high in search engine rankings… but good content will ensure that you rank high in SERPs and that users can find your content. What good is a beautiful website, if it doesn't even appear in search results?

"Only good content can bring qualified visitors to your site; more qualified visitors means more quality leads."

But content is not just for search engines! It's primarily created for the visitors of your website. Content should be written keeping the users in mind, and not necessarily the search engines.

Here are a few reasons why good content is so important, in generating leads for your website:

Content provides information

The main purpose of content is to provide useful information to the users. Content is written to answer the questions that users are querying about. Hence, you should write content to address the needs and queries of your users.

For example, let's say that someone searches for information on how to calculate his taxes. He comes across websites that provide relevant information, and he will choose an article that provides in-depth knowledge about calculating taxes and covers all the bases.

Visitors come to websites either looking for a product/service or to otherwise get information. Simply offering your product or service isn't enough here; you need to provide relevant information about those products/services as well. Keeping with the example above, if you're selling a tax management software, then providing information on it will get more users to buy your software.

Quality Content Provides Value

Well-written content ensures that users remain engaged in your website and that they come back for more. To retain users, nothing is more powerful than content. And if someone feels that your content provides value to them, they will also go on to share your content with others.

Let's consider the coronavirus situation. We all know it's a deadly virus that is fatal in many cases. But if you were to write an article which states that the virus is dangerous, then it serves no value to the users, because everyone is aware of that fact. However, if you had content on how to take necessary precautions to avoid contracting the coronavirus, then it would be of great help to users, and it would benefit everyone.

So ultimately, you are increasing your website and traffic - and as a result, this will generate more leads, which was your whole goal in the first place!

Content attracts qualified traffic

Quality traffic is a more important metric, compared to overall traffic when measuring the performance of your website. Quality traffic consists of those website visitors that are more likely to convert to leads than others.

A great way to target qualified traffic is by writing content that caters directly to their unique needs. They will have a high interest in what you have to offer and have a high chance of converting into leads.

These users usually stumble upon your website through organic searches, in which they search for a particular topic, and your website has the content they are looking for. Creating content to cater specifically to these users seems like your best bet in increasing conversions.

The content demonstrates your authority and expertise

In the previous point, I mentioned that most of the traffic you're going to attract with content marketing will be from search engine results pages. The better your content is, the more traffic it will attract.

Take our company website, royex.ae, for instance. We specialize in web and mobile app development - but how do we show our authority and expertise to our visitors? By creating high-quality content on these topics that consistently rank high in search results! This content is shared and linked by many across social media, and inside our articles, we offer solutions to the problems faced by the users.

The content shows how your services can help

Continuing the example from above, among our high-quality content is a "How to develop apps like this" series, in which we explain the development process and costs that are involved in prominent apps that are being used by millions of users.

Through content like this, we can help users who want to develop apps similar to those popular apps – and at the end of each of these articles, we link our service page to show them how, by acquiring our services, they can achieve their goals. Ultimately, it's all focused on helping the users.

How to Create Content for Every Stage of the Buyer's Journey

A person doesn't immediately become a customer. They will go through a three-stage process called the "sales funnel", which consists of the stages a customer goes through, before finally making the purchase.

This process begins from discovering your website, subscribing to your email list, talking to a sales rep, and then deciding whether to buy from you. Through content marketing, customers can get engaged during the various stages of their journey.

Here, understanding your customers is of the utmost importance. If you fail to do this, there will be a gap between you and your prospective customers. The content that you publish must be relatable to your readers, or else they might leave you.

You have to put yourself in their shoes. Consider how they think, what they think, what kind of answers they're looking for, and what kind of solution they would accept. Once you have the answers to these questions, you can craft your content accordingly, so that it aligns with their needs.

I have already defined the three-stage buyer's journey: awareness, evaluation, and purchase. Now, in this chapter, I will discuss them again, but within the context of content; how you can create content for each stage of the buyer's journey.

Top of the Funnel: Awareness

At this point, a buyer is trying to solve problems, get an answer, or meet a need. They're looking for top-level educational content to help direct them to a solution, like blog posts, social content, and ebooks. Their value as a lead is low because there's no guarantee that they'll buy from you. But those who find your content helpful and interesting may just journey on into the middle of the funnel.

Middle of the Funnel: Evaluation

When someone moves into the middle of your funnel, this means you've successfully captured their attention. They know they have a problem that has to be solved, and now they're trying to discover the best solution. As they're evaluating their options, the need for a future purchase commitment creeps up.

While the top of the funnel is designed to educate a prospect, this is the stage where you want to show why your solutions, in particular, are the best fit. (You also want to help people determine if they're *not* a good fit, which will be very important later on for healthy customer retention. If you convince customers who aren't a good fit for your business in the long run to buy, you could very well be shooting yourself in the foot, in the form of a high churn rate later.)

The middle of the funnel is typically a point of extended engagement, in which you're nurturing a lead, building a relationship, and establishing trust between the audience and your brand.

Bottom of the Funnel: Purchase

"Leads at the bottom of your funnel just need that final nudge and that compelling call-to-action to get them to make a purchase decision"

The bottom of the funnel is where someone is making the actual purchase decision. They're ready to buy, but that still doesn't guarantee that they're going to buy from you. That's the last choice they have to make: where do they get the solution they're seeking?

In most cases, leads at the bottom of your funnel just need that final nudge and that compelling call-to-action to get them to make a purchase decision. At this stage, the right offer and content can have a dramatic impact on lifting your conversions.

Content Ideas for Each Stage in the Funnel

Content Ideas for the Awareness Stage

Consumers nowadays are very well-informed. More than 80% of them do some kind of online research before they make a purchase. They actively look for answers to their questions and issues related to the products/services that they are interested in.

For this stage, you mostly have to focus on content that is optimized and well-written. You can include content such as educational articles, blog posts, ebooks, and research reports. You might also opt for some interactive media here, such as videos, infographics, etc.

Let's consider the example of drones and quadcopters, which are a type of unmanned aerial vehicle. These are still relatively new pieces of technology, and not many users are aware of how to set up a drone and use it.

In the awareness stage, most of your content should be aimed at making the users aware of this device and how it can benefit them, how to use it, etc. The content must be educational and informational, with no mention of buying drones, because the users are still new to this.

Content Ideas for the Evaluation Stage

For this stage, you must aim to build a personal relationship with the buyer and to nurture them. Blogs are a great way of driving traffic to your website, but they won't be able to help you build that personal touch and engagement.

Buyers are focused on evaluation and filtering out options that don't work for them. The businesses that have a clearly-defined strategy for this stage can get up to 10 times the response, compared to companies that haven't yet defined the stages in their sales funnels.

For the people who are in this stage of the sales funnel, you need to prove your expertise and authority to them. You need content like expert guides, interviews, white papers, and webinars that highlight your benefits and advantages compared with your competitors.

Bringing back the example of drones, during the evaluation stage, you can create content that compares and contrasts different types of drones that are available. The users are now aware of this, and now they need to know which one to go for - so making your product stand out from all the competition should be the goal here.

The more detailed your write up is, the higher your expertise and authority will be. So make the user sway to your side during this stage.

Content Ideas for the Purchase Stage

The bottom funnel offer won't guarantee you turning leads into customers - but if done right, it will compel the buyer to close, deal, and convert.

The types of content you should be focusing on are case studies, trials, and demos. Many companies offer free trials to their premium service for a limited time – and once the trial period is over, the buyer will find it difficult to let go of it, and will go for the full service.

Considering the above example, the user has evaluated all his options and is ready to make a purchase. In this stage, your goal is to push or nudge the buyer to make that final purchase decision. You will need to offer content with a compelling and convincing CTA at the end so that they feel inclined to go for your drone. With the right offer and content, your conversion chances will increase dramatically.

Create a More Engaging Buyer's Journey

The sales funnel centered around the buyer's journey is unique for every business, and as such, you cannot copy someone else's sales funnel and expect it to work for you. So when you create your own buyer's journey, you need to keep a few things in mind.

There is a general formula that needs to be followed: understand your buyer and their needs, develop your sales funnel based on your industry and the buyer's needs, and devise a well-crafted content marketing strategy that maps content to each phase of the sales funnel specifically.

If you do this correctly, this approach will greatly enhance your relationship with customers and ensure maximum customer conversions.

Types of Content in a Website

Blogs

Blogging has always been a staple form of content on a website, and businesses have long used blogs to attract and engage traffic.

But the times have certainly changed, in the way that these blogs are written. It is now the relevant, well-written, and detailed pieces that can attract the attention of your readers. Blogs are a great way of building trust, authority, and relationships with your readers. Most importantly, they also help convert these readers into buyers.

Modern blogging practices also ensure that these blogs are written in such a way that they are easy for search engines to find. In other words, they are SEO-optimized and friendly content, which is especially shareable on social media.

To make sure that you keep your readers engaged, put a routine schedule into place for yourself, posting blogs every couple of days. These blogs must be interlinked with each other to help readers discover more about you. Add a CTA in each post, as well, to increase your conversions.

Listicles

Listicles are those list articles you see that usually begin with a number in their title (for instance, "7 reasons to invest in real estate"). These types of content are extremely popular and always rank high in search engine results.

Readers find these articles easy to understand, scannable, and organized. They are also highly shared and referred – and on the publisher's side, they're also easy to write. Once you have a topic in mind for one of these articles, you just need to determine the number and then focus on writing about each section individually.

To master the skill of writing great listicles, you must make sure to research and organize your content first. You need to number your subheadings, and the number should match the number in the title. As with any other content, your keywords must also be relevant.

These articles get a lot of clicks when combined with a catchy title. Just make sure the title and the content match!

Ebooks

As the name suggests, ebooks are simply books put out in a digital format. They are a long-form of content and are usually available as PDF downloads. They are phenomenal methods for sharing your expertise on a single topic in depth.

Ebooks are used by businesses to generate leads, in the form of free downloads in exchange for the recipients sharing their contact information. They can also easily serve to establish authority and increase your content spectrum.

When writing ebooks, make sure to provide solutions for a particular problem. The audience must be able to read it and feel that they gained something from it. You need to invest quality time in researching and organizing your content, for this.

Of course, there is no definite, set length that your ebook has to be; it can range from a few pages well into the hundreds of pages! It all just depends on the scope of your topic, and how in-depth you decide to cover it. Make sure and divide your ebook into multiple chapters, along with relevant headings, images, and proper formatting.

The cover of your ebook is also something you should take time and consideration in designing. The title and visual design you use will be a huge deciding factor, in attracting readers.

Infographics

Infographics are images that contain a lot of information, such as statistics, research, data, findings, etc. They are a very popular form of content that tends to get shared around more than other types of content on social media.

A good infographic represents its information in an organized, presentable, and easy to understand format. You can either include these in your articles to supplement your content or as standalone content.

Infographics are usually long, high-resolution images that have a lot of information in them. If you opt to include these in your content, you should always make sure the information and graphical elements are not cluttered, and that there is enough space between the elements.

Choose a font that's easy to read, and pick out a color that aligns with your brand.

Videos

Videos are increasingly becoming most people's preferred form of content. More than 80% of all web traffic is in the form of videos, and for good reason!

Videos allow you to digest a lot of content in a short amount of time, and it takes a lot less effort to sit back and watch a video, compared to reading an article. Videos are proven to increase conversions, and more than 75% of consumers are likely to purchase after watching a video on the product/service.

Videos come in many forms and may be presented as educational videos, interviews, reviews, presentations, explainers, and more.

When creating a video, your main aim must be to provide value and answer the doubts and issues of the viewers. You can do this by providing the appropriate information and addressing their pain points.

Don't make it an ad for your brand. Make the viewer feel like they are gaining something from watching your videos, and then just include a CTA at the end to direct them to your website. You can embed these videos in your relevant articles, or upload them to popular video sharing sites like YouTube. It's up to you!

How-to Guides

How-to guides are a form of instructional content that explains a concept or a task in great detail. They are written to share your knowledge with users who are looking to learn about a particular topic.

These guides are excellent opportunities for exhibiting your knowledge, expertise, and authority. At the same time, they also help you to build trust among your readers, as you prove your expertise to them through this content.

You must take extra care when writing these guides to ensure that they are clear, concise, and accurate. The reader must find it easy to understand and absorb the information easily. Breaking your content down into different sections is probably a good idea, here. You can also include images, diagrams, and videos to make the content more interesting and interactive.

How to Write Good Content

To write good content, you first need to know what good content is. The basic criterion of good content is that it should serve its purpose.

Good content must also answer the questions of the users, retain the traffic it attracts, and, ultimately, it must lead to more conversions.

"The basic criteria of good content is that it should serve its purpose."

Suppose you've written an article - the basic purpose of this content is to rank in Google, and once you get traffic, those users should stay and read your content. Let's say you've written a few lines for a banner, where the purpose of the content is to get users to click the banner. If the content serves its purpose, then, we can say that it is good content.

Centering your content around your readers is the best way of ensuring that your content increases your conversion rates. You cannot simply write generic content that is no different than what already exists out there, and then expect your traffic and conversions to increase.

Here are some proven strategies that will help you write high quality, converting content that your readers will positively love:

Pick your topic

Choosing a topic can be a truly daunting task – and coming up with a content idea is quite tricky, without a system in place.

For this, you'll need to start keeping a list of content ideas beforehand. You can research what type of content your audience is interested in, and you can follow what type of content others are posting - and whenever you get ideas, write them down on your list.

"Centering your content around your readers is the best way of ensuring that your content increases your conversion rates"

In most niches, coming up with an entirely new and unique content idea is quite rare. It takes genuine time and effort - so it's also completely okay to work on an existing topic by giving it your unique take, and add something new, to it.

Researching your content

Now that you have your content topic, your next step is researching the topic, to gain as much knowledge about it as you possibly can. Just sitting down and writing about something, without having done any of the prerequisite research, is a big mistake, and in all likelihood is going to result in poor content.

Your first step should be to find out what is already written on the topic. You can accomplish this via a quick Google search. Pick out the first five or six results, and have a look. After all, the content in these results must be well-written, for it to rank so high!

Take a glance at these articles and single out the common themes that are covered inside them. You can keep these themes in mind when you're writing your article. This doesn't mean that you should copy their content. That's plagiarism, and it is highly frowned upon, and not SEO-friendly, either.

You are merely doing this for idea generation. Another important thing to note here is the ideas that none of these articles have covered, which you can then add to your article and enhance its value.

Do keyword research

Keyword research involves finding out what popular phrases and terms people are talking about and discussing.

Writing on topics that are trending or popular will make sure your content reaches out to a lot of people. To do this, you need to include the keywords found from your research in your article.

You have to place them naturally, and not stuff them in forcefully where they don't fit. If you do, this will only hamper your search engine rankings.

Writing the content

Once your research is done, it's time for you to write your post! You should decide the title of the content first and then proceed to write the post itself. Keep the following in mind, before you begin:

- o Length, readability, and format of your content
- o What your users are looking for
- o Use relevant images and video

Use different text formatting tools, such as italics, bold, bullet points, etc. to highlight important points. The post length of your content depends on how deeply you're going to cover the topic. Generally, longer content tends to rank better.

Most importantly, write your content as if you are directly speaking to the reader. When they read your content, they must find the answer to what they are looking for, and they must also be engaged.

Remember that you are writing this content to add value to the user, and not for any other purpose.

Optimize your content

Once you have your post all written out, now it's time to optimize it! So far, you have written the content keeping the reader in mind. Now, you have to optimize it, keeping SEO in mind - and more specifically, on-page SEO.

The reason why we want to optimize our content is to get it to rank better in search engine results. Here are some of the things you need to make sure of when doing on-page optimization:

- o   Meta description includes your main keyword
- o   Heading and subheadings contain the main keyword
- o   Relevant interlinking to other content in your website
- o   Outbound links to authoritative websites

o   Images must contain alt text

You will find more information on this in chapter 4's On-Page SEO section.

How to Write Great Blogs

"Some content will go viral, generating tons of hot traffic to your blog, while other content will be lost in the archives. If you want more of the first kind, you've got to put your readers first."

~ Neil Patel

No matter what kind of online business you run, you need to blog for a variety of reasons. Some of them include:

- o Driving traffic to your website
- o Increasing your SEO rankings
- o Promoting your brand and increasing your authority
- o Developing better customer relationships

But all of this only happens when you write great blogs! Great blogs should serve two purposes: the first is that they rank high in search engines and attract a lot of visitors, and the second is that they must retain those visitors, with them spending time reading your content, instead of bouncing off to another website.

Let's look at how you can start writing truly great blogs:

Great headlines grab attention

One of the biggest mistakes blog writers make is that they will write their post first, and *then* come up with a headline.

But without a headline, there is no definite structure to follow. The content goes off-topic and misses the market with readers, leaving them confused and irritated.

Take your time to craft a headline that works to clearly state the purpose of the blog and attract readers at the same time.

Once you have your headline ready, you have an effective roadmap to follow for your blog, thus resulting in an article that is well-received by your readers!

Your headline must promise the answer that the users are looking for. After all, it's all about them and their needs.

Write an Introduction That Grabs Attention

With a great headline, you have successfully lured users into reading your blog. But now what? Now, you need a catchy introduction to make them read your content!

Your introduction section is the first thing that most readers will read after they've opened your blog – but if your introduction isn't unique, catchy, and relatable, they'll leave. You don't want that.

So, to glue your readers right from the start, write an introduction that captivates their attention. Instead of taking a formal tone, which quickly bores the readers, try and go for a more personal approach.

"If your article introduction isn't unique, catchy, and relatable, the reader will leave."

Write your blog as if you are speaking directly to them. You must make them feel an emotional attachment to you, and the best way to accomplish this would be to show them that you understand and relate to their problem.

Think about things from their perspective and point of view, and then write your introduction.

Provide value in your content

At this point, you've gotten readers to click on your blog, they have read your intro, and next, they're going to scroll down below and read the rest of your material.

The rest of the content comprises the subheadings and the text inside of them. Subheadings are great because a reader can quickly identify what a particular section is about, just by reading the subheading.

Write your blog content uniquely and interestingly. Don't just follow what everyone else is doing. Have your style of writing that sets you apart from the rest!

List important information in bullets, so that you can make the information concise and clear. Include vibrant images which complement your content as well, to keep things interesting.

And finally, be generous in your posts. Offer your readers a lot of value, so that they'll want to come back! These returning readers are going to eventually become your customers, one day.

Close with a Motivational Bang

Once you have written your main content, it's time to draft up a good conclusion. This is the point where you motivate your readers to achieve the goal that was promised in the blog's heading.

"Be generous in your posts. Offer your readers a lot of value, so that they'll want to come back!"

By showing them that you believe in them, they will feel connected to you and will be motivated to take action. Your conclusion must make them feel the need to do something about the issue or the problem that they face.

Show them how they can achieve their goal with you and your brand. This is how blog posts can tremendously help increase conversions.

Chapter 6

Website Redesign Strategy

Website owners might go for a redesign because their existing website design isn't working for them, and they need a design revamp. But you might wonder: what role does strategy have to play in a website redesign? All that matters is that the site looks good, so why strategize?

Many simply go in without a plan, when redesigning their website. They spend a lot of money on a new CMS and website layout, thinking that their new, modern-looking site is going to effortlessly bring in a lot of conversions and new customers for them.

But when they launch their new site... their sales don't increase. In fact, in many cases, their sales plummet! Why do you think that happens? It's all because they lack a clear-cut strategy when it comes to website redesign.

A website redesign strategy will clearly state what you want with your online presence. A good redesign strategy will state what site elements must be present and how to present them and will ensure that whatever redesign is applied will effectively lead to customer satisfaction and happiness. Ultimately, it should generate leads.

Why do you need a good website redesign strategy?

A website redesign can be an extremely challenging and exhausting process. The vast majority of website owners out there are reluctant to get their website redesigned, because they've had bad previous experiences.

The common issues they face are long redesign duration, technical problems, and low success rates. The whole process can also end up costing the company more than they'd planned, and that money could have been utilized elsewhere.

This is because, when you start a website redesign, there could be a lot of mistakes you might commit that could be easily avoided. It takes proper knowledge and experience, to get the job done properly.

"Every 18 months or so, small- to mid-sized companies need a website redesign, to adapt to the changes."

The other issue is that some website owners only get a redesign to improve the looks of their website, but they don't focus on other factors that contribute to sales and conversions.

Even if your website used to perform great in the past - and it even does well in the present - as time passes, you'll likely discover that it isn't doing so great anymore. This is because design trends change, and so do user preferences.

Not only that, but search engine algorithms also evolve, and your website needs to be re-optimized for that. Every 18 months or so, small- to mid-sized companies need a website redesign, to adapt to the changes.

If your site lacks traffic, is unable to generate leads, and has a low sales record, then you need a website redesign. But redesigning without a strategy will only fail, and this why I'm going to lay down a website redesign strategy for you. This strategy will revolve around the source of traffic, as there are four: organic search, paid search, social media, and direct traffic.

Four main sources of traffic to your website

Not everybody visits your website directly. As you know, users arrive at your site from different sources, of which there are four main routes: organic search, social media, paid traffic, and direct traffic. In this section, I will explain how you can center your website redesign strategy based on the source of traffic.

> *"Your website redesign strategy must be based on the traffic source."*

Organic Search

Organic-search traffic is the type of traffic that generates from users coming to your site via search engine results. These are the people who actively search for solutions to their problem - the problem that can be solved via your product or service.

For instance, let's say a person who needs handyman service for his home types in "Best handyman service near me" into a search engine, and your site appears as one of the search results. He visits your site by clicking the link. This kind of traffic is a perfect example of organic traffic.

How visible you are to search engines depends on the strength of your SEO. The higher your rankings are in SERPs, the higher your organic traffic will be.

Paid Search

The traffic that comes from the clicks to your ad campaigns, such as PPC, is paid traffic. If you run an ad campaign on Google or a similar platform, you pay for every click on the ad that is posted on that platform.

The traffic generated from this source is valuable because users see the ad and it interests them. That means that whatever you are offering, they are willing to acquire it.

Social Media

The traffic that generates from users who click on your social media posts which redirect to your website is called social media traffic. Popular social media websites such as Twitter, Facebook, Pinterest, LinkedIn, Instagram, etc. are all great for traffic generation.

You can also run paid social media ad campaigns, which will be able to reach out to a lot of people and drive a lot of traffic to your website. Websites like social bookmarking sites fall under this category.

Direct Traffic

Some users visit your website directly by typing your website's URL into the address bar; they already know about your website and the services you offer. This kind of traffic is referred to as direct traffic.

"Your direct traffic numbers indicate how strong and popular your branding is."

Your direct traffic numbers indicate how strong and popular your branding is. If these numbers are going up every month, this means that more and more people are learning about your brand.

You must strategize your website redesign considering all four sources, to get the most out of your website redesign. Hence, the following strategy for a website redesign is going to consider all these traffic sources.

Redesign Strategy based on SEO

The target of this strategy:

As the traffic originates from search results, this strategy is based on how to appear on these search results. It may not be possible to rank for every keyword on the first page of Google, and not all keywords are important for your business. Your objective is to find the best keywords for your business. Start with keyword research to find the necessary ones, then fill up the important meta-information that is required for search engines, prepare your content to support those keywords, and then link your content internally.

Keyword research

You should start your website redesign with keyword research, which involves finding out what keywords users are interested in and searching for. Once you have your keywords, next you have to incorporate them throughout your website. All of your content must have relevant keywords in their headlines and body paragraphs so that it's easier for them to rank high in search engines.

Meta information

Meta information (or metadata) is simply information about other information. It is the information that you see in search engine result pages that are listed organically. Important SEO meta information includes page title and meta description.

You need to include your seed keyword in your titles and meta descriptions so that it's easy for the search engine to find your content. This will tell them what your content is about. Well-written titles and meta descriptions will grab the attention of users and increase your traffic.

Body content

Like we discussed with web content in the previous chapter, this is where your main content resides - including text, images, video, etc. High-quality content ranks high in search rankings, so take your time when creating your website content.

You need to take certain factors under consideration, like keyword choice, frequency, density, placement, and spacing, to fully optimize your content for SEO.

Internal site linking

When one of your posts links to other relevant posts of your website, that's what's known as internal site linking. This is an important component of SEO and helps search engines to crawl your site in a better, more efficient way.

Internal linking also helps your website by decreasing the bounce rate, increases the time users spend on your website and boosts your ranking for the keywords that you link.

Redesign Strategy based on Social Media

The target of this strategy:

Here, the traffic originates from social media, and you need to optimize your website to obtain the maximum visitors you can from social media. To accomplish this, you need to have some social media-centric design elements on your website. This involves making your social pages visible on your website through icons and CTAs, allowing social logins, allowing your content to be shared on social media, and embedding videos on your website.

Let Customers Know What Social Media Sites You're On

When redesigning your website, link all your social media on your website. They must be visible on your homepage, either on the footer or the header, so that your social media can be found easily.

Make those social media icons visible and stand out! Social networks like Facebook, Twitter, Instagram, Pinterest, YouTube, LinkedIn, etc. are quite popular, and these icons will allow for more interaction and connectivity.

On every page that you have content on, be sure and include the "share" and "like" button so that your readers can share the content if they find it useful. This greatly increases your exposure and reach, and brings in even more visitors.

Include a CTA that asks visitors to "like" your social media pages, such as Facebook, follow you on Twitter, or join the discussion on LinkedIn.

It is better to design these social media icons yourself so that you can make sure they match the look and feel of your website, and don't look out of place. These small details all add to the aesthetics of your website!

Allow Social Logins, to Make It Easier to Connect With You

Social logins will allow your users to log in to your site from their social media accounts so that they won't need to set up an individual login, and allows sites to create a community and connect.

Moreover, allowing users to login via their social media is convenient for them, and takes a lot less time. They also increase the conversion rates for user registrations.

Make Content Shareable

What if your website has killer content that your readers find helpful and share-worthy, but there is no option there for them to share it? This is a big mistake, as having the option to share your content to different social media websites has become extremely important.

By not allowing your users to share your content, you are severely limiting your exposure. But you can remedy this - give them the option to tweet, pin, or discuss your article. Place the share buttons where you find the most suitable.

Embed YouTube Videos, When Appropriate

YouTube videos embedded on websites help them rank higher in search results - especially if you have a lot of videos.

Videos increase the view time on your page, as well as improve your conversion rate. They're also fantastic for supporting your text, adding a sense of interactiveness and variety.

Redesign Strategy based on Paid Traffic

The target of this strategy:

The main target of this strategy is to generate the maximum amount of traffic with the least amount of investment. This strategy involves redesigning the landing pages to make them optimized for traffic and lead generation. Keep the page visually simple, include media on the page, choose proper colors, make your page responsive, and finally, write content that serves the purpose of the landing page.

For paid traffic sources, you would run a paid advertising campaign like Google AdWords, in which you choose your desired keywords where you want your ad to show up. Then, for the number of clicks that users perform, you pay Google accordingly. You need to monitor how many clicks you are getting, to measure your ad campaign's success.

The webpages you create for these ad campaigns are known as landing pages. When redesigning your website, you might also consider redesigning your landing pages, if they are not currently performing well. Here is a comprehensive redesign strategy for landing pages:

Keep the landing page visually simple

Visual simplicity takes all the elements of a landing page's UI into consideration. A minimalist design is important for landing pages because this will help visitors focus on the offer at hand.

Landing pages are designed for one single purpose: to convert. Therefore, cluttering up this page with unnecessary visual elements is not a smart choice, and would only serve to distract the user. Here's how you can keep your visual design simple:

- Have a lot of whitespace in your design, so that users can focus on CTAs.
- The key features, such as CTAs and forms, must stand out from each other visually.
- The design creates a contrast between elements, to highlight them even further.
- The page is designed in such a way that it influences the user to stay on the page and to keep scrolling and reading.

Include media in your landing page

Along with text, make sure to also have media on your landing page. Including some appropriate images and videos can help in convincing readers to act upon the CTA. Through the use of images and videos, you can effectively tell a great story, highlight your product/service, and establish a personal connection with your audience.

Make your images, as these will help build trust and relationships with the visitors. Avoid stock images at all costs, as they are bland and generic, and will not reflect your brand personality.

Videos improve user engagement and are excellent for SEO. They are great for explaining the features of your products and services, and so, it's a great idea to include them on your landing page.

The Importance of Color

"There is no single color that works for everyone.
You need to find out what works best for you."

Colors play a large role in human psychology, and can even dictate how we feel and act. And so it's only natural that the right color combination can improve the looks of your landing page, and even influence conversions! Here are some tips for using colors efficiently in your landing pages:

o Combine opposite colors to create contrast, to increase readability and make the elements stand out.

o Segment your colors depending on demographics. Different cultures prefer different colors.

o There is no single color that works for everyone. You need to find out what works best for you.

Create a responsive landing page design

Responsive design has been the standard for quite a while now. These days, it is hard to find a website that isn't responsive– and landing pages are no exception. They must have the same UX and UI on mobile devices and full-screen layouts.

Consumers these days often prefer shopping from their mobile devices, and they account for a major share of web traffic. If these landing pages are not optimized for mobile devices, then, you will be limiting your sales a lot, since no one likes browsing on a page that isn't responsive.

Content – The Foundation of a Great Landing Page

The content of your landing page decides whether or not the visitor wants to convert with you. Yes, your landing page is *that* important! Here are the best practices for creating content for landing pages:

- o **Attention-grabbing headlines:** These are the first things that visitors are going to see when they visit a landing page - so be sure to craft a great headline to make a great impression. Your headlines are either going to pull the visitor in or make them leave the page.
- o Make sure to include the unique selling proposition and the main message in your headline, so that your readers know what to expect.

o **Great CTAs:** Call to action buttons are one of the key elements of a truly successful landing page, and act as a gateway between the user and your product/service. Improve your CTAs by emphasizing the main CTA, to make it easy for the users to act upon it. Use visual cues to indicate the CTA. You can also use bright colors to highlight the CTA buttons, compelling the user to click on them.

o **Use People in Landing Pages:** Use of people on your landing page will help build trust and increase conversions, due to the psychological impact it has on consumers. Smiling faces instill confidence and get the user to think about the offer at hand. Use real people that consumers can relate with. They help build a personal connection and have the user connect with you emotionally. And these emotions will eventually trigger a response from them.

Redesign Strategy based on Direct Traffic

The target of this strategy

To qualify as direct traffic, visitors must be aware of your company and website, and then type it directly into the address bar. Hence, the focus of this strategy is to increase your branding. For this, you can utilize visual elements like logos, colors, and characters, have enough whitespace on your website, keep your fonts simple, express your story, and use relevant images.

Since direct traffic is all about users knowing you and your website URL, you can start increasing your direct traffic by improving your branding. When you redesign your website, you can apply certain strategies that will also boost your branding. These strategies are discussed here:

Visual Elements to boost branding

Visual elements (such as colors, logos, and characters) can make your brand stand out. The combination of these visual elements all comes together and gives your brand a unique personality.

For instance, you might use a brand mascot in your marketing endeavors. These visual elements will make your brand memorable among people, and will also add a distinct flavor to your brand.

An Attractive Logo

Your company logo is an integral component of your brand's web design. A good logo will have an innovative design, attention-grabbing colors, and just the right proportions.

Logos are associated with your brand, brand values, vision, and mission. An attractive logo will always linger in the minds of consumers. For instance, Coca-Cola's logo is known worldwide and is instantly recognizable.

Balance White Space

Whitespace has a visual appeal that is very pleasing to the eye and removes clutter from your website. Having whitespace between blocks of content highlights each section, and works to increase readability.

To enhance the visibility of your logos, images, and other content, having some whitespace is key. Research has shown that whitespace improves comprehension by 20%.

Simplify Your Fonts

Gone are those days when "Times New Roman" and "Courier" are the only fonts you'll find being used on a website! On the contrary, there are many beautiful fonts available out there, that you can use to make your website look unique and appealing.

Some of the fancier fonts can make it hard to read what you have to say to your users, however, so be sure and keep the font simple and easy-to-read.

Tell Your Story

Telling the personal story of how your brand started gives your brand a personal touch. Adding this to the "About Us" section of your website will give a great feeling of history and backstory to your brand.

Adding the images of the key employees in your company and giving a brief bio on them all adds an extra layer of trust and connection with your audience, as well, and ultimately promotes your brand even further.

Use Relevant Images

Put some effort into improving the quality of the images on your website. I talked about avoiding stock images before, and I will certainly repeat it. They are not good for your brand. Instead of using them, hire a professional photographer who takes great photos, or hire a designer that creates great images, that can reflect the personality of your brand.

Chapter 7

Website Page Structure and Elements

So you have a business website running… but are you sure that it's optimized for generating you sufficient leads? Does it have all the elements a website needs, to fully maximize conversions?

There are a great number of elements that go into a website, and it can be hard to know which ones are working and improving your performance.

"Good content increases your authority and trust,

and is an absolute must, for any website to excel in

leads"

What Needs to be Considered For Website Design

We have already discussed web design in the previous chapters. To optimize your website for lead generation, you need to keep certain things in mind, when designing it.

If you don't, you might still get traffic to your website - but in the long run, you won't generate leads and sales. So, how do you design your website to make it a high-performance lead generator?

"Your brand's image and personality must be considered before you begin the website design process."

Here are the main things you have to consider when designing a website:

1. Who is it for?

The first question you need to ask yourself is, who are you designing this website for? What kind of audience are you targeting? What demographic is going to be interested in what you have to offer? For instance, if you design a website to sell branded sneakers, you'll go for a sporty, trendy design that resonates with the youth.

2. What will be the structure of the website?

The next step is to determine the structure of your website, which is a blueprint. Starting from the homepage, you need to map all the other pages of your website to it. By creating a site map, you will know the pages of your website, and how they will all be connected. Each page will link to some important pages, such as the homepage, contact page, and about page. You also need to determine the scale of your website, and how you plan to increase it in the future.

3. Making mobile a top priority

You should design your website while keeping mobile at the front of your thoughts. More than 50% of all web traffic originates from mobile devices, and that number is only going to keep rising over time. Ensure responsive design for all the pages of your website, so that they are optimized for viewing on mobile devices. The mobile view must look the same as the full-screen layout view.

4. What images to use

Images play a role in website design, and you need to carefully consider which images to use on your website. Invest in a good photographer to take professional photos, which will be placed throughout your website. You need to choose images that reflect your brand, and to avoid stock images at all costs. You should also make sure that the images are optimized and compressed, to enable faster loading.

5. Brand

Branding and website design both go hand-in-hand. Website design is centered around your brand so that the design brings out and represents your brand. Some brands out there only have an online presence - and so, for them, a website is the only visual representation of their business that exists. Your brand's image and personality must be considered before you begin the website design process, to ensure synergy between the two. Here are a few aspects to consider:

- o Do you have a logo to use?
- o This is where you might want to start, as you could then use elements of the logo to begin structuring the brand image.
- o Which font are you going to use?
- o Don't use overly fancy fonts that make it hard to read your content. Use a simple-looking font, which makes the text readable, while at the same time standing out.
- o What about color?
- o Colors have the inherent ability to influence human psychology, and thus you need to use colors that reflect your brand, and that your audience can relate with.
- o What about any design elements?

o   Design elements (like icons) can greatly enhance the visual appeal of your website, and you should use them wherever possible. Design your icons, rather than using pre-existing ones.

6. Usability

Usability is an integral part of your website design. Whether it be functionally or visually, you need to have consistency in design. There are visual elements such as buttons, hover modes, menus, etc. that you all need to consider individually. For example, if all your clickable elements are rectangle-shaped, then your buttons must be rectangles, as well. However, you may also opt for rounded shapes, as they are typically considered superior in web design. In terms of menus, you have to consider good usability, too. For example, hamburger menus look great, but in terms of usability, header navigation is far superior. At the end of the day, a good design has to be usable.

7. Layout

The layout of a website refers to how you organize your images by placing the elements in an organized manner. A good layout will have a good balance of multimedia elements and text. You should aim to keep your layout simple and to avoid clutter and congestion. Ensure that there is enough whitespace between the elements, to give everything a clean look. You might also consider wireframing the website before you design the actual interface, which will allow you to make changes easily since you have a solid base.

8. Selecting the right CMS

CMS (Content Management) is a software that is used to manage and create digital content on a website. You need to choose the right kind of CMS, that allows you to customize your design completely. Choosing the wrong CMS can result in utter disaster for your website. Thankfully, there are many readily-available CMS and custom CMS options out there to choose from! Two of my recommended CMS would be WordPress and Umbraco.

The Best Way to Design the Important Website Pages

Homepage

Your homepage is the very first page that a visitor sees when he visits your website. It is also your website's most-visited page.

It leaves the first impression on your visitor's mind, so your job is to do exactly that. But it's not just about visuals, here. The main goal of your website is to convert. You need to give the users an incentive to convert here, or else they won't.

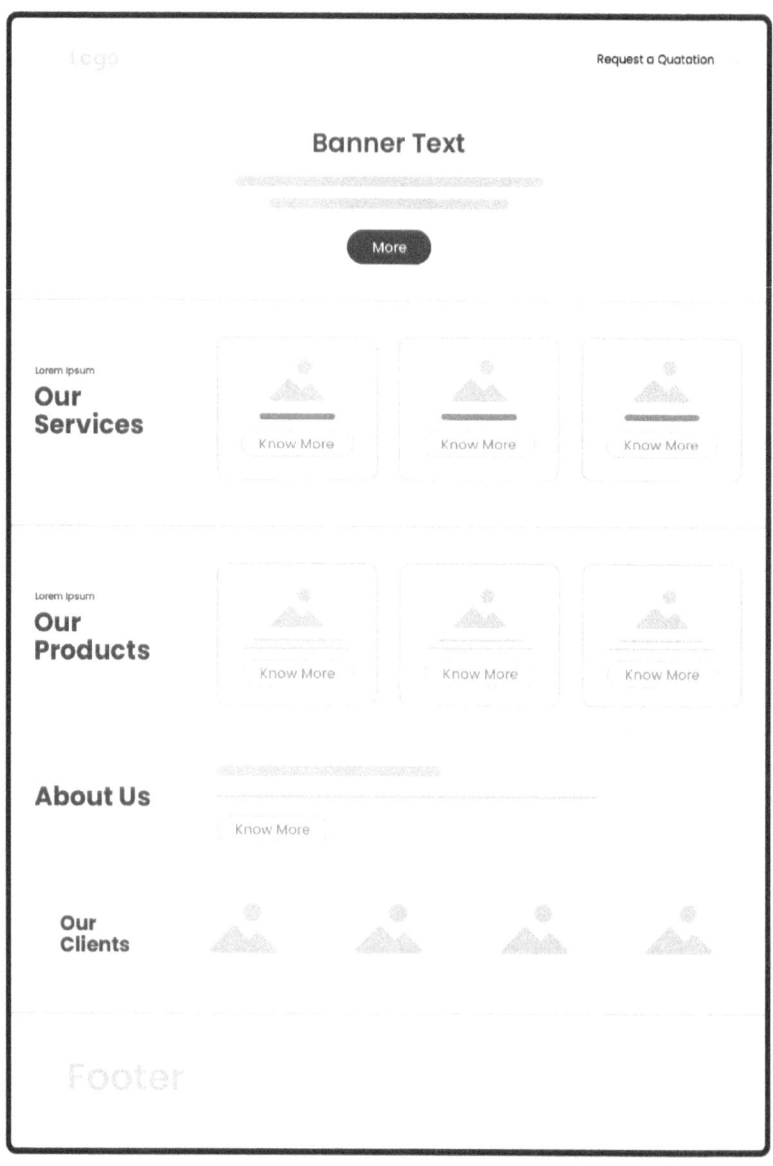

Image: Sample Website Home Page

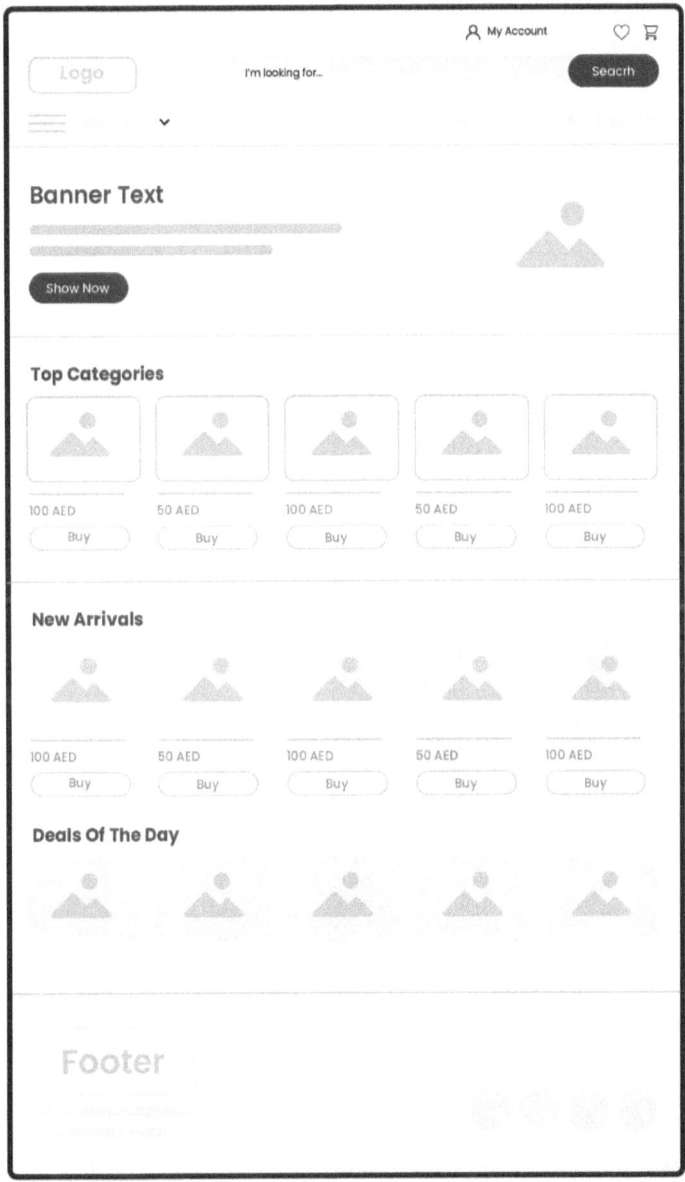

Image: Ecommerce Website Home Page

To do this, you need to make the site intuitive and easy to use as possible. There are elements that every page needs to have, for that to happen successfully. Remember that consumers come to your website for a reason.

They are either interested in your product or services, or they have come to read your articles. Either way, your job is to direct the consumer to the page they want to visit. The homepage must be designed in such a way that navigation to any other page is both seamless and convenient.

If the user finds their homepage experience positive, the chance of them converting increases. Here are the best practices, when it comes to designing a homepage:

Contrasting colors: Strong and contrasting colors will make your website elements stand out.

Loads fast: Research says that if a page takes any more than 3 seconds of loading time, users will begin losing their interest.

Good navigation: Navigation must be designed in such a way that it feels easy to traverse around the site with ease.

Mobile-friendly: Your site must adjust to the mobile screen and feature a proper layout, just like it has on a computer screen.

Relevant calls to action: The CTA you use must contain strong, compelling words to get your visitors to click. They must also stand out from the other elements, to put proper emphasis on them.

Engaging: A good combination of visuals, layout, design, and content can all get the user to stay, and later return for more.

What should be on the Home Page:

- o Logo and branding elements
- o Navigation
- o Headline
- o Call to action
- o Social Proof
- o Photos
- o Footer

What should not be on the Home Page:

- o Excessive pop-ups
- o Long blocks of text
- o Hide Links
- o No whitespace
- o Videos set to autoplay

About Us

Next to the homepage, your "About Us" page is the second-most important page of your entire website. It allows your users to get to know a bit more about you and your business. But simply stating your company information along with a couple of other details isn't enough, here.

This space is a chance for you to tell your unique story! Rather than writing a boring description like every other website is doing, you should instead aim to talk directly to your readers and describe your company's origins. Talk about how your company started from humble beginnings and made it to the position it is today.

When you approach it this way, you earn trust and credibility. Talk about the team behind your company's success, and highlight each of their roles and importance to the company. Bring about the unique selling points of your company here, and explain it to your readers.

Don't try to sound too professional and smart. Keep it simple, and make the visitors appreciate your products and services. The more your customers can learn about you, the stronger your relationship with them will be.

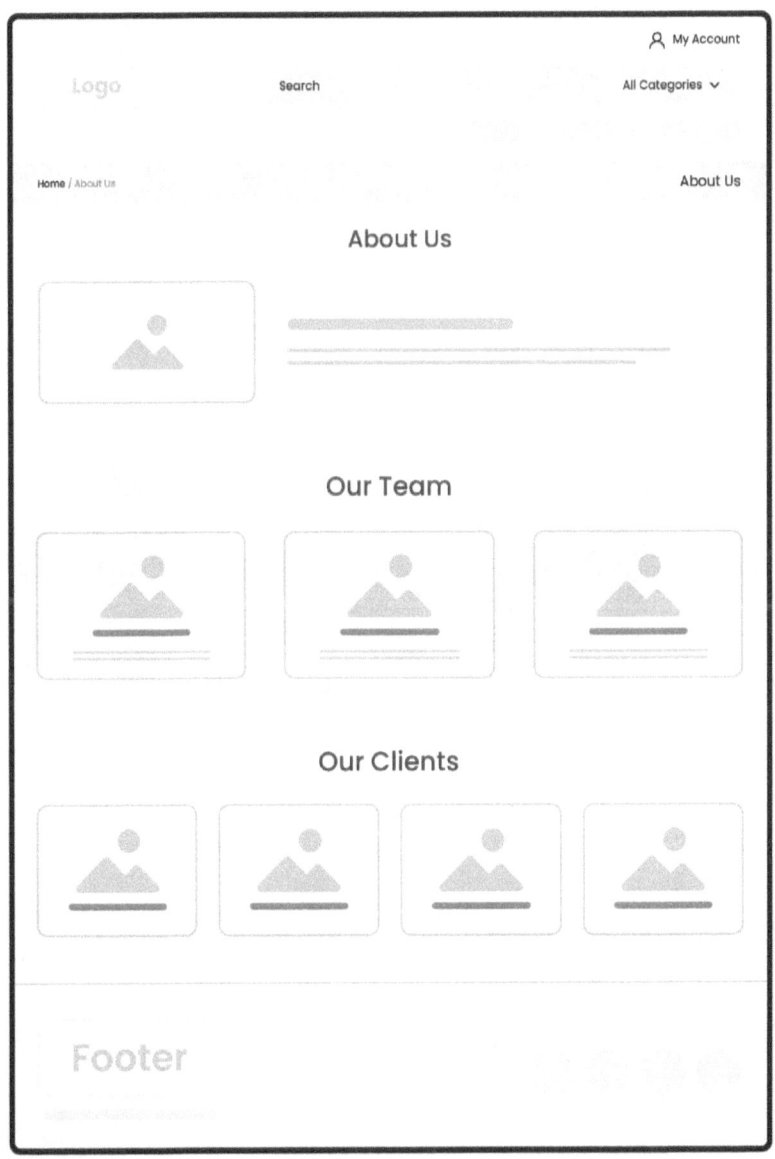

Image: Sample About Page

As time passes, and as your company grows in size and strength, you'll need to keep this page updated. The About page is one of the greatest, most surefire ways to build trust with your customers, so make the most out of it!

What should be on the About Us Page:

- o Establish a mission statement
- o Outline your company story
- o Explain who you serve
- o Explain what you're offering them
- o Describe your values
- o Introduce the team behind the business

What should not be in the About Us Page:

- o Hype
- o Sales pitch
- o Too much information
- o Excessive design

Contact Us Page

The Contact Us page is also one of the most valuable and important pages of your website. It is through this page that the visitors and customers of your website can get in direct contact with you. But simply including the necessary information and forgetting about it isn't all you need to do, to ensure that your Contact Us page is in great shape.

This page is the biggest call-to-action on your website - and you need to design it like that. Whenever a new visitor browses through your website and is interested in your products or services, they will likely want to contact you to discuss further. If they need assistance on any issue, they will head for this page.

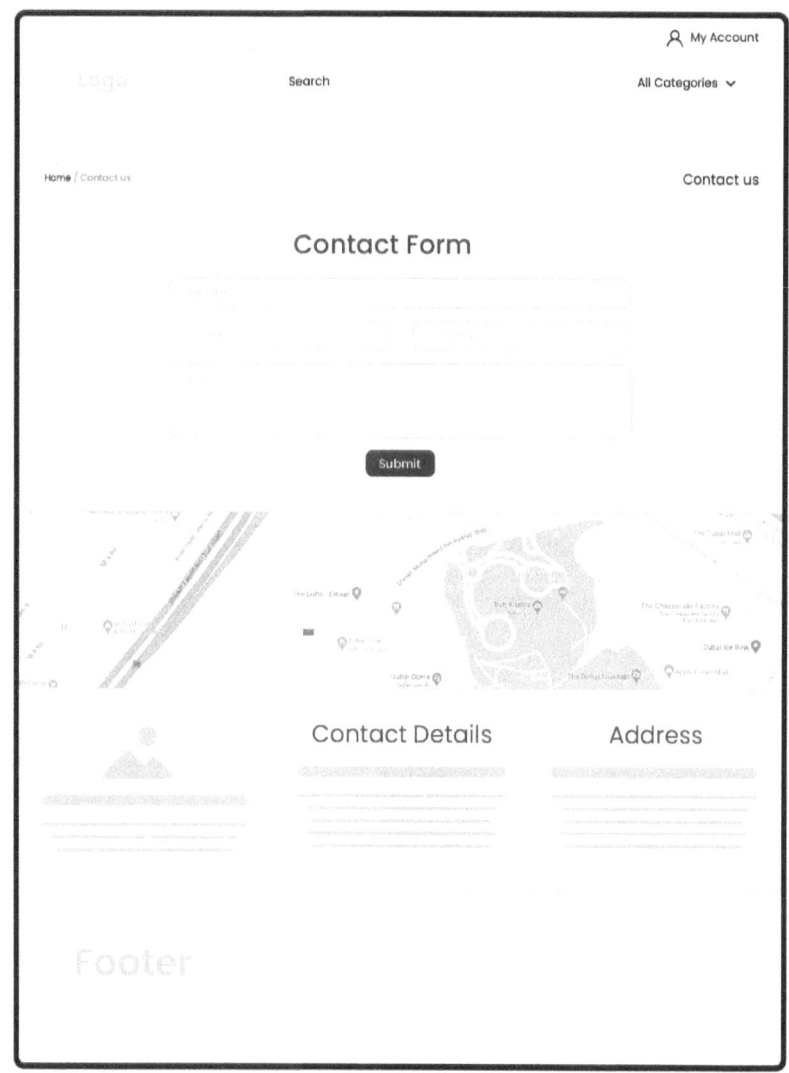

Image: Sample Contact Us Page

Thus, you must design this page by keeping the goal of converting in mind, efficiently presenting the information. Here are the guidelines you need to follow, when you design this page:

o   Start with some text explaining why the user should get in touch with you, and then compel them to do so.

o   Aside from contact information, leave out any excessive or unnecessary information. Let the focus be on how your users can communicate with you efficiently.

o   Don't ask the user for unnecessary information. Keep the form fields minimalistic, and don't ask questions you don't need the answers to right away.

o   Offer multiple modes of contact, giving flexibility to users. These modes can include phone, live chat, filling out a form, and email. They can choose whichever method they prefer.

o   Add your physical address and real contact information. This adds trust and credibility to your site.

o   Give the users an estimate of when you can get back to them. The response time doesn't have to be pinpoint; a close estimate, along with the assurance that you will contact them back, is enough.

What should be on the Contact Us Page:

o   Physical address
o   Email address
o   Telephone number

- o   Contact form
- o   Chatbox
- o   Time zone
- o   Operating hours

What should not be in Contact Us Page:

- o   Confusing elements
- o   Hide contact details
- o   Other company information

Portfolio page

A portfolio page is where you display your previous work, show your skills and strengths, and is particularly helpful for websites that offer services. They can easily showcase their services for previous clients here, so that prospective new clients can view them and judge their work.

But simply jamming all your projects and work into this page isn't going to work for you. There is a certain way to design this page that will lure potential clients and convince them to avail of your service. Let's look at the best design practices for a portfolio page:

Your Best Work Comes First: Many websites make the mistake of displaying their work in the order of completion, i.e. they show their latest work first, and the rest of the list follows. And some even do it worse - by randomly displaying their previous projects. Both of these practices are wrong.

What you should be doing instead is displaying your best projects first. This is what the clients are going to see first, and you have to impress them within this limited time window.

Create a Portfolio that is Easy to Navigate: To fit in as many projects as possible on the first page, many websites leave very little space between them, and with no division between them either. This is a huge mistake.

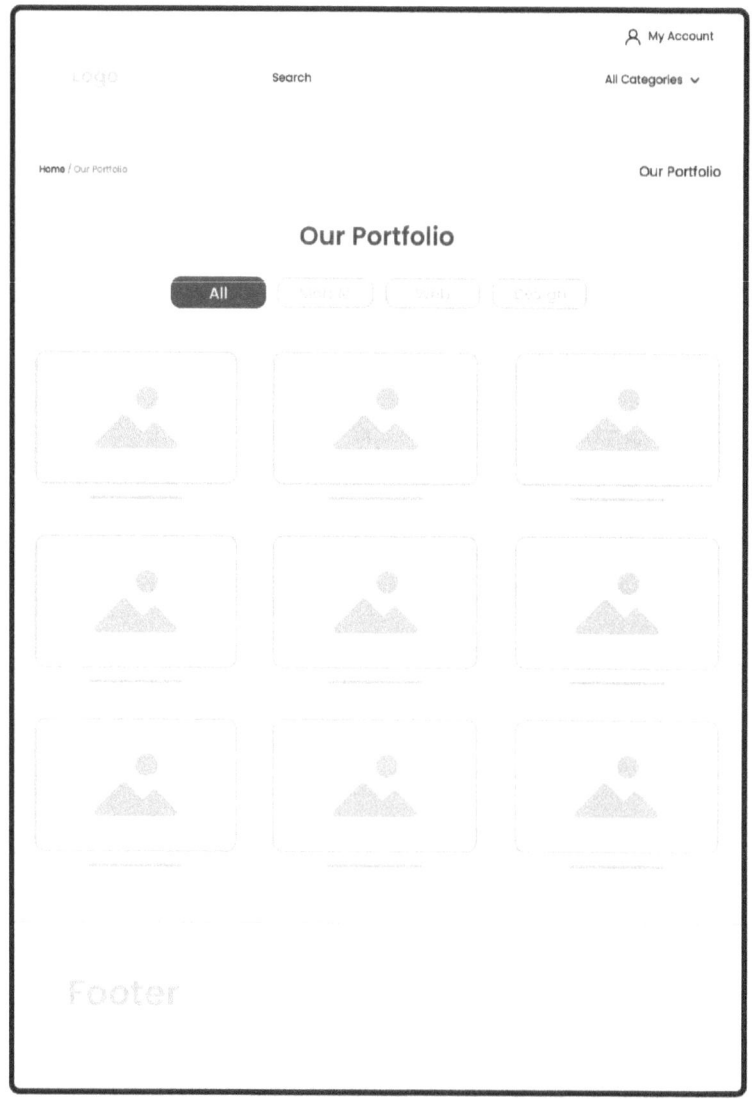

Image: Sample Portfolio Page

You need to leave enough space between each portfolio, and navigating between them should be completely hassle-free.

To make it look more organized, you could divide your portfolio into various categories and segments, so that it's much easier for clients to browse through your work.

For example, in our website, royex.ae, which is a mobile app and website development company, we have categorized the portfolio into four categories: website, mobile apps, e-commerce, and others. This makes it much easier for our clients to browse through our work.

Choose Projects with Best Results: If you are starting new, and have still only served a few clients so far, it's okay to display all your previous works - as you don't have that many yet.

"It's okay to be selective and display a few of your best works, rather than cluttering up the page with all your projects."

But if you are a veteran in the business, and you have many years of experience, your portfolio is going to be massive. You don't have to display all your work, in this case. Some projects are quite insignificant, and adding them here won't impress your potential clients.

It's okay to be selective and display a few of your best works, rather than cluttering up the page with all your projects. You can also talk about what kind of projects you would be interested in working on, in the future.

Tell the Story – Provide Context: For every successful project, you have completed, add a little story, and explain how the work was accomplished.

Adding context goes a long way in explaining your thought process behind the projects that you undertake. And if you want to go the extra mile, you can even add case studies that explain the process of completing that project.

What should be on the Portfolio Page:

- o   Your best work
- o   Simple layout
- o   Easy navigation
- o   Testimonials

What should not be on the Portfolio Page:

- o   Blocks of text
- o   Lack of client information
- o   False information

Product Page

Your product page design will say a lot about your website, and therefore, you must pay special consideration when you're designing it.

Customers and visitors spend a lot of time on this page, and you have to design the page with them in mind. You must optimize this page so that it can be found easily, it has enough information about your product, and that it is well-designed to provide the customer with a great online shopping experience.

The following guidelines will help improve the possibilities of people finding this page easily and increasing your rate of conversions:

Answer these questions in your product description

A detailed and accurate product description is very important for your product page. It satisfies the customers, and it is great for SEO, as well. Simply stating the manufacturer's information is a bad idea; your product page won't even rank in search results if you do that.

To write a great product description, be sure, and answer the following questions in it:

What is it?

Start your product descriptions with this. Explain what the product is, especially if it's a new product on the market.

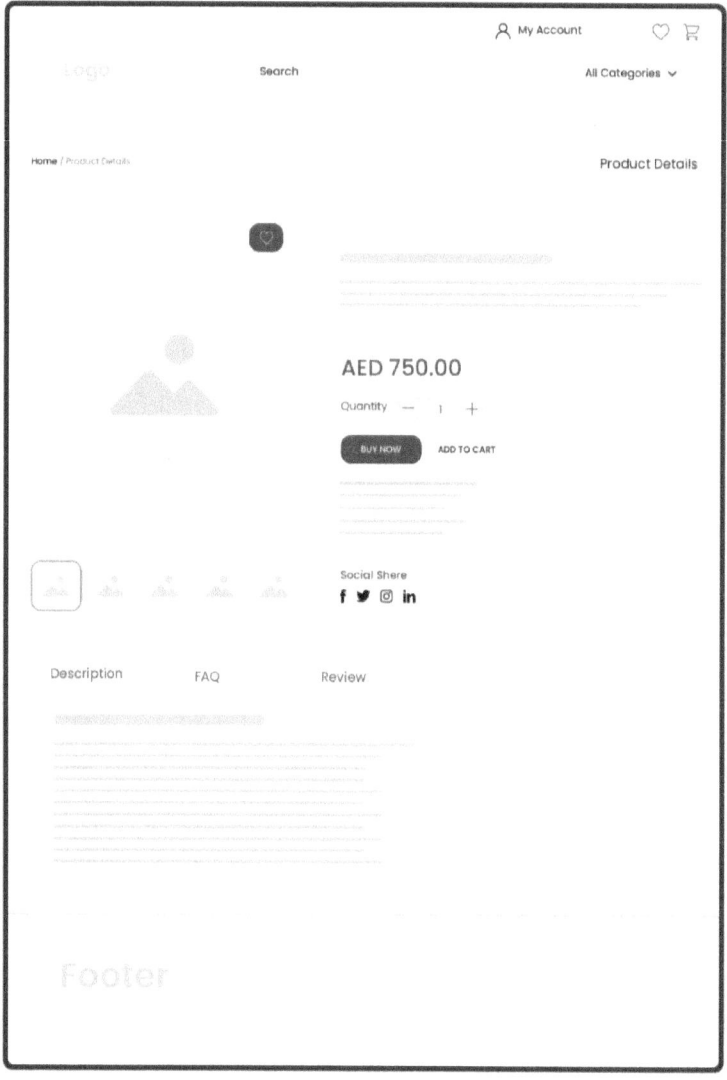

Image: Sample Product Details Page

If your customers are looking for a particular product, then this is what they'll want to know first.

How does it solve the problem?

What problems does your product solve? How will the user benefit from it, and how will it solve his problem? These questions should be answered in the description.

Users appreciate it when you answer these questions so that they won't have to now enquire about it separately. Inadequate information is often the reason why someone won't go for your product.

Why your product?

You have addressed what your product is and what problems it can solve... but unless your product is extremely rare, there will likely be many available alternatives to your product on the market.

So why should consumers go for your product, and not just any of the other alternatives they have access to? You should answer this by stating the reasons why your product is superior, compared to the rest of the competition.

List all the unique features of your product, and highlight all the things your product is capable of that the other products aren't.

What is it made of?

Finally, add all the metadata for your product. This includes all the materials or ingredients that went into making the final product.

Adding this information adds more transparency and details which might interest your shoppers. This extra information is also great for search engines, as it provides more context.

Create Great Product Images

Product photos are what customers see when they first land on a product page. Great images can form a great first impression in the minds of the users, whereas poor images can cause them to perceive the product negatively.

Not only do product photos supplement the product description, but they also add more details that the text doesn't. Images have more psychological impact than text, and therefore, great images will naturally help you sell more.

But how do you create great product images? You need to start with good photography, by taking professional pictures of your product from multiple angles. You can edit your images to give them a vibrant, appealing look. Just remember to also optimize the images so that they don't slow down your loading times!

Keep Your Product Photography Consistent

To ensure uniformity in your product photos, you need to maintain consistency between them. This makes it easy to search and compare various products, as well as enhances the professionalism of your brand.

How can you achieve consistency in product photography? Keep the background the same for all of your product photos (preferably white). Use the same image dimensions and aspect ratio for all of your photos. Optimize the images for SEO, mobile, and zoom.

What should be on the Product Page:

- Concise product description and specifications
- Clear product images from multiple angles
- Filters to sort
- Clear price descriptions
- Product reviews
- Clear CTA
- Product comparison

What should not be on the Product Page:

- Long, unclear product descriptions
- Low-resolution product images
- Inconsistent color schemes

Service Page

The service page is where you list out all of your offered services. This is also one of the most highly viewed pages of your website, and you must treat it as such when designing it. With the right content and layout design, you can dramatically improve your sales.

The aim is to tailor this page to appeal to your target client and niche. By doing this, you will be attracting the people who need your services. Here's how you can design a high converting service page:

State the obvious: Give an overview of all the services you offer, and create a separate page for each service, where you explain them in detail.

You should list the advantages that your prospective customers can benefit from after availing of your services. Another effective way of getting your users to convert is to highlight their problems and then explain how your services can solve them.

Include Testimonials: Have a section on your website where you add user testimonials. Past clients that have availed your service and are satisfied with it will happily give you their success story, after using your service!

Image: Sample Service Details Page

Their glowing references about you will inspire confidence and assurance among your new, prospective clients. They will now know what to expect from you and what your business can deliver based on their needs.

Be Transparent With Your Prices: I mentioned earlier in this book that you need to be transparent with the prices of the products or services that you offer.

With services, your price may vary, as per the client's requirements. In that case, listing out the actual price can be tough – but at the same time, a close estimate of the cost should also be able to help the user.

This way, the customers who value your service for the price charged will contact you, and those who cannot afford your services won't waste your (or their) time.

Include a Call to Action: This one is a must, for a service page. The visitor knows about your service, and they know how other clients have benefited from it. They also know how much it is going to cost them to avail of these services.

Now, the final step is to offer them a CTA that says "Get a quote", or "Contact us", so that you can get potential customers to contact you, and you can both come to terms to meet their needs.

What should be on the Services page:

o Brief descriptions of services

o FAQs related to services

o Relevant images

o Benefits of services

o CTA buttons

o Pricing information

What should not be on the Services page:

o Using technical buzzwords

o All services in a single page

o Generic, unresearched service descriptions

Cart Page

About 70% of all customers abandon their carts in online shopping sites, according to a study. This means that 7 out of 10 people will leave their cart completely behind, even after adding items to it. This may happen on your website, too, if you are not careful with the cart page.

To avoid this, you need to follow some guidelines and avoid some bad practices, when it comes to designing a good cart page.

Follow the CSF Formula. The CSF formula states that your shopping cart should be:

Clear: Only display the important information on your cart page, such as items added, quantity, price, pictures, etc. Remove any unnecessary clutter from the page.

Simple: Use simple language and design on your cart page. There's no need for any fancy elements that will distract the user from proceeding to checkout.

"7 out of 10 people will leave their cart completely behind, even after adding items to it"

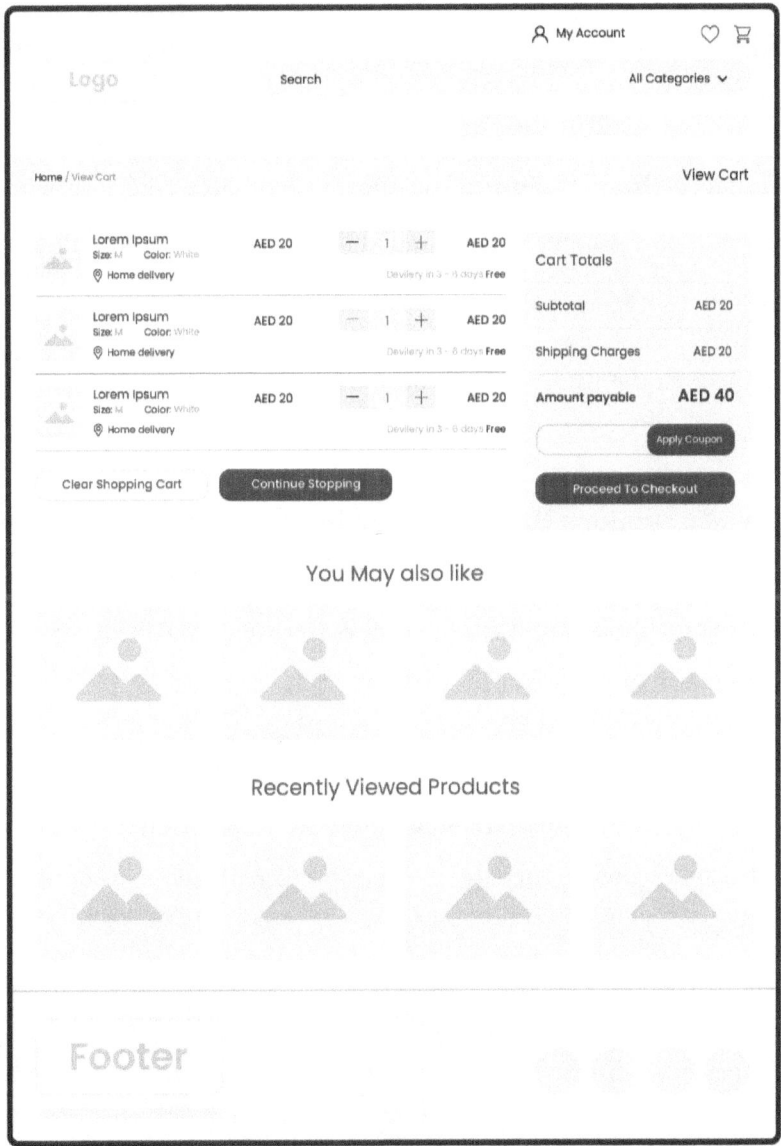

Image: Sample Cart Page

Fast: By keeping the cart page clear and simple, it will naturally be fast. The fewer time visitors spend here, the less there is a chance of them abandoning their cart.

Detailed Product Summary: On the cart page, the visitor checks whether all the items they've added are present or not and in the right quantity. From here, he will proceed to pay.

Display all the order information, including the name, quantity, size, images, etc., so that they don't even have to leave the cart page.

Payment options that your users love: Different customers prefer different payment methods. And in this day and age, multiple payment options are a must, or else you run the risk of losing your customer to some other business.

By offering users their favorite preferred payment methods, you are reassuring them and increasing conversions. Nearly half of shoppers will cancel their purchase if their preferred payment option isn't available.

If you run an international store, you should also keep in mind what people from different countries prefer to use as payment options.

Continue Shopping Option: If the customer wants to leave the cart page to add more products or check out something else, they'll have to abandon the page.

To avoid this inconvenience, a "continue shopping" option can be implemented on the website, which allows users to browse around the website while still saving their cart.

They can then continue from where they left off, once they come back. Keep in mind that many users also use the cart page as a "wish list" to store future purchases.

What should be on the Cart page:

- o Order modification options
- o Order summary
- o Product image
- o Shipping cost
- o Estimated time of delivery
- o Order cancellation

What should not be on the Cart page:

- o Forcing users to sign in
- o Absence of a "continue shopping" option
- o Best offer from other vendors
- o Confusing offer

Checkout Page

There are many reasons as to why shoppers might leave the checkout page - a bad experience while checking out, being forced to create a user account, security concerns, payment option issues, high shipping rates, etc.

You can avoid all of these issues by following these measures when designing a checkout page:

Shop without a user account: Some websites require the customer to register for an account when placing an order. This practice may annoy one-time shoppers and ruin their entire user experience on your site. However, if you just let them shop without entering their details, they may be pleased with the experience, and may then even return as regular purchasers.

Eliminate Distractions: The checkout page is designed to get the users to pay by entering the relevant information and then leave. Any unnecessary distractions should be removed. You might even consider removing the header and footer section of your website.

Remove Unnecessary Form Fields: Nobody likes to fill out long forms that take a ton of time to complete. To this end, only ask for mandatory information from the users and nothing more. If you still want to obtain some extra information, mark those questions as "optional", so that users don't have to fill them if they don't want to.

Home / Checkout

Checkout

Returning Customer? Click here to login

Name

E-mail address*

Phone number*

Country*   Town/city*

Street address*

Create an account?

Name

email address*

Phone number*

Country*   Town/city*

Street address*

Cart Totals	Total
Subtotal	AED 20
Shipping Charges	AED 20
Amount payable	**AED 40**

Payment method

Cash on delivery

Online Payment

I have read and accept the terms & conditions

Place Order

Logo

Search

All Categories ⌄

My Account

Footer

Image: Sample Checkout Page

Remind Users What They Are Buying: Add a summary of their order, which includes product details and relevant photos to give a reminder to users. This enables them to confirm their order, and also removes any hesitation about the order.

Let Customers Edit: It's only natural for customers to make changes to their order. If they want to change something about their order on the checkout page, then give them the option to do so. If they find that they've made a mistake, or changed their mind, and then learn that they have to start all over, they might feel frustrated and give up on your site - and possibly even leave a bad review. It's also a good idea for you to give them the option to remove any item from the order and save it for later. Maybe they don't have the budget to afford it right now, but they can come back later and get it when the time is right.

Make the Checkout Look Secure: To assure customers that all your payment processed are secure, add some security, such as an SSL certificate. Simply adding it is not enough - you need to add a security logo which indicates and ensures the users that all their payments on your website are 100% secure.

What should be on the Checkout page:

- o   Security seals
- o   CTA button
- o   Payment methods

- o Editing order
- o Save Cart option
- o Live chat support

What should not be on the Checkout page:

- o Unnecessary items
- o Sign in to checkout
- o Excessive form fields

Thank You Page

A thank you page is a special page on the website that visitors, leads, customers see after filling out the form on the landing page or any other page which includes a form field.

Once the visitor has filled out the relevant information and gets converted to a lead, you don't need to do anything extra - but displaying a thank you page is going the extra step to acknowledge the efforts of the visitors and confirm the offer for them, which they originally filled the form out for.

Image: Sample Thank You Page

Image: Sample Thank You Page

Here's how you can design a fantastic thank you page:

Message: The user has filled out the form on your website to avail of an incentive, such as an ebook or a report. So, once they've arrived on the thank you page, you can display a nice message like: "Thank you for applying for the free offer. Your ebook is now available for download."

Display your site's navigation menu: Additionally, you can put a navigation menu in place, just in case the user wants to get back to your website and continue browsing. This is a good thing, and you must provide them with every opportunity to stay on your website.

Provide additional content: You can also link to important content on your website that will interest them. A thank you page that also offers resourceful content will be quite different from most other thank you pages and will leave a lasting, positive impression on the visitor's mind. Make sure not to spam too many links, though - as then, the thank you page will lose its purpose.

Include your social options: Plug your social media on this page, because this will give them a chance to connect with you on more channels. If you display them as icons on the side, they won't take up much space and will help you connect with your users on a personal level.

What should be on the Thank You page:

o   Message of gratitude

o   Referral message

o   Link to your most popular content

o   Product recommendations

What should not be on the Thank You page:

o   Irrelevant text

o   Lengthy post

Search Results Page

There are two kinds of search result pages: one is for e-commerce websites, which displays the search results for products, and the other is a content search result page, which will display relevant content - such as articles and blogs for the keyword searched.

The image below is a great example of a ecommerce search result page. If your website isn't an e-commerce website, you won't need a product search result page. One example of a content search result page is the search page on royex.ae, where you can search for any content by entering a keyword, and then we use Google to display the search results.

This is a crucial element of the search experience and allows users to search for content on your website readily. Accurately displaying search results adds to the overall positive user experience, and so you must put special emphasis on designing this page.

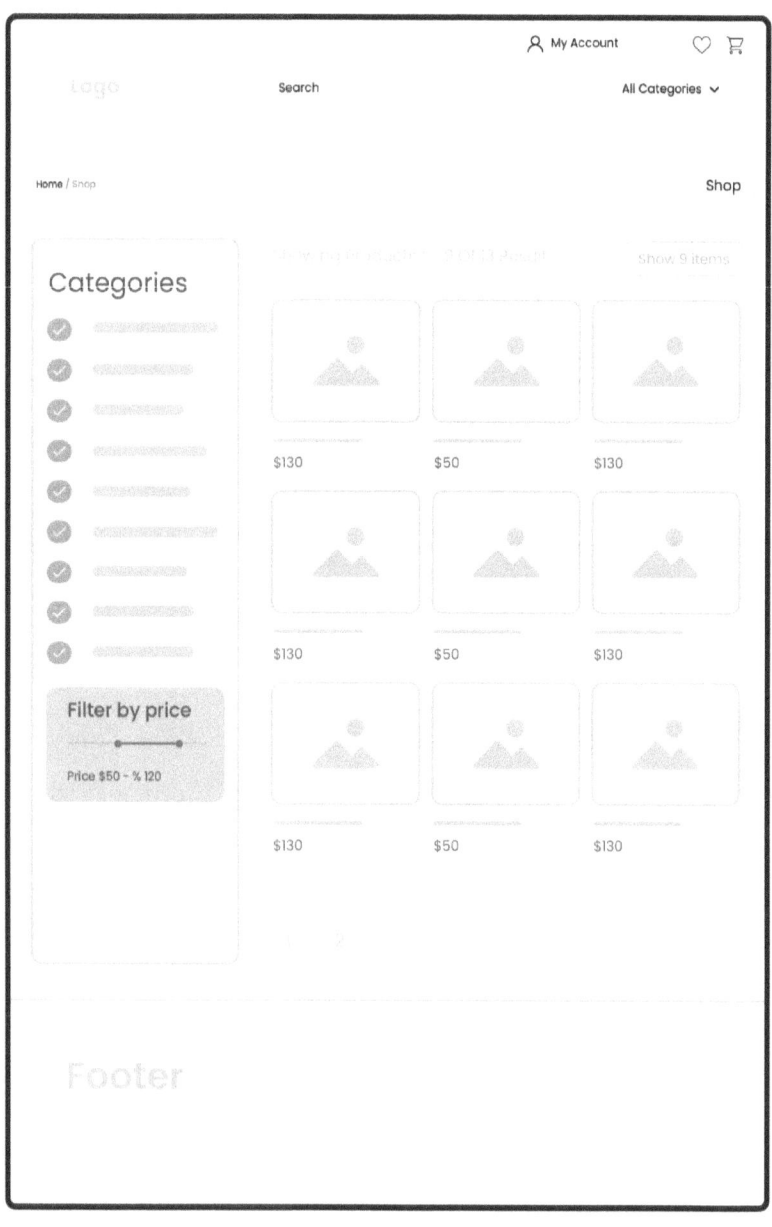

Image: Sample Ecommerce Search Result Page

Image: Content Search Result Page

Here's what you need to do, to design an optimal search results page:

Don't erase users' queries after they hit "search": If the users input something in the search box, hit "search", and don't get the results they are looking for, they may want to go back and modify their original query slightly. But if your website completely removes their original input, now they have to type it out all over again, making the whole process harder and more irritating for them.

Provide accurate and relevant results: This goes without saying, but you need to display results that are exactly what the user is looking for. In this case, the first page is important, as the majority of the users don't go beyond that. Ideally, the first three results should satisfy the user's query, so that they don't have to scroll further. For the user to trust the search tool, it must consistently return accurate results.

Use effective autosuggest: As soon as the user starts typing, autosuggest (true to its name) can begin suggesting words that might add up to what the user is looking for. As they continue typing, you can make the suggestions dynamic, so that they change with their ongoing input. This must occur instantaneously, or else they won't rely on the suggestions.

Correct typos: Humans are prone to making mistakes, and typing errors are certainly no exception. If they make a mistake, detect this and suggest the correct term instead. You could also display the words they intended to search with in the first place. This avoids the user having to retype anything, and is, therefore, a positive experience for them.

Show the number of search results: As the results are displayed, show the number of search items generated, so that the users can estimate how long they want to go through the results page. If there are many results, they might want to rephrase their search to get exactly what they are looking for.

Keep recent user's search queries: Store the user's recent searches so that, if by any chance they re-search the query again, it is already displayed to them. When they place the cursor on the search query field, you can also show them a list of their last five search results.

Choose proper page layout: There are two types of layout through which you can display your search results: grid view and list view. A basic rule is to display details with a lot of text in the list view and display pictures (such as product pictures) in the grid view.

Provide sort and filter options: Give the user the option to sort and filter results based on various relevant criteria. Users can select one piece of criteria or multiple, and the search results must be dynamic as the filters change.

Don't return "no results": If the user's search query cannot return any relevant results, don't simply display a blank page, as this can be extremely frustrating for users. Instead, what you can do in cases like these is provide them with alternatives.

What should be on the Search Results page:

- o Autosuggest

- o Alternative suggestions

- o Sort and filter options

- o Customized result page layout

What should not be on the Search Results page:

- o "No results"

- o Remove user query

- o Static results

Landing Page

As we discussed in detail in earlier chapters, landing pages are designed for one purpose: conversions. Hence, every design element of this page must be focused on increasing conversions, and nothing else.

Their job is to attract visitors and influence them to proceed down the conversion funnel. For this reason, there must be no distractions (like external links) to divert the visitor's mind. A minimalistic design that is free of clutter and only contains elements that will help in conversion is optimal, for landing page design.

Sufficient whitespace and contrasting colors are also an important element for landing page design. Make these pages short, with minimum scrolling, so that the user doesn't have to scroll too much to get to important elements like the CTA button.

Additionally, interactive media, such as images and videos, are a great addition to landing pages. Not all users like reading long paragraphs; whereas videos and images can convey the same message in a more catchy, concise manner.

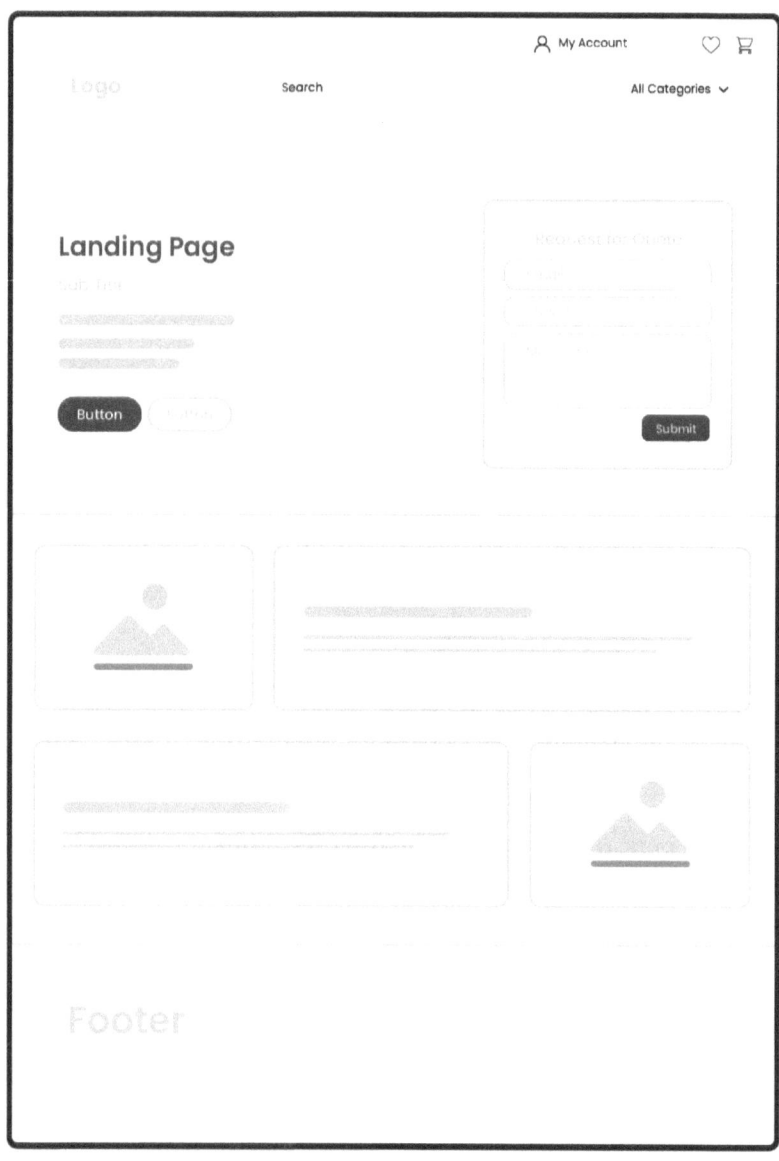

Image: Sample Landing Page

To get your brand to stand out, you need to ensure consistency in colors and elements of the landing page. But this doesn't mean that this page looks the same as all the other pages of your website. Keeping the landing page design unique, while also maintaining your branding, should be your goal here.

What should be on the Landing page:

o   Attractive headline

o   Images and videos

o   Enough whitespace between elements

o   CTAs that stand out

o   Design that maintains branding

o   Value proposition

o   Contact form

What should not be on the Landing page:

o   Unnecessary links to other pages

o   Long scrolling pages

o   Redirects

o   Excessive information

Blog Landing and Details Page

The blog landing page is where you will find all the blog posts of a website listed in an organized manner, usually chronologically. This page must be designed in a manner that pleases both the users and the search engines.

It must contain important elements if you aim to make the user experience pleasant. For instance, there must be a search bar in the above section, so that the user can easily search for a particular blog post, rather than having to scroll and navigate between unfamiliar pages to find it.

You can either implement this search yourself or enable Google to search on your website. In my experience, Google search works better in most cases and is usually more accurate than manually implementing a search function.

Blogs are usually written covering various topics - even for websites that cover a particular niche. So, you should categorize your blogs according to the topic, so that you can make it easier for users to find blogs covering their interests.

For each post, give a summary on this page, along with a button that will take them to the full post. This gives your visitors an idea of what the blog post will talk about. And as time goes by, the number of blog posts on your website will keep increasing, and it will become more and more difficult to display them all on a single page.

You could enable infinite scrolling to show all the posts on a single page, but you should avoid this, as Google cannot crawl through all the pages when you have this feature enabled. Instead, use pagination, where you list the posts on numbered pages that start from 1, and then keep incrementing.

What should be on the Blog Landing page:

- o Search bar
- o Pagination
- o Posts sorted by categories
- o Date of publication
- o Author name

What should not be on the Blog Landing page:

- o Infinite scrolling
- o All blog posts listed together

Image: Sample Blog Landing Page

Image: Sample Blog Details Page

There are certain things to keep in mind when designing the blog details page as well. The blog details page contains information on a single topic. To start things off, you will need a feature-image for the post that will illustrate the topic that you want to cover. The heading is probably the first place where the reader will focus on. The heading design must be clear and eye-catching. The font size of the title must be large enough and an attractive font must be used.

The majority of the blog will the content that you write covering the topic. But that doesn't mean you should only include text. It will make the blog boring to read.

Make sure to include images and videos to support your content. Divide the text into blocks of paragraphs to make the article easy to read and make it look organized.

At the end of the blog post, include a section for author bio. Include the name and image of the author and add a short bio. Keep a comments box to encourage feedback from your readers.

This will make your blog more interactive and help you connect with the readers. One final thing to do is add a "Similar article" section where you can list similar blog posts to keep the readers engaged on your website.

Give an option to share your article on social media by including social buttons such as Facebook, Twitter, Pinterest, etc. Another good practice is you can ask the reader to subscribe to your newsletter so they get notified every time you publish a new post.

What should be on the Blog Details page:

- o A title that stands out
- o Text in paragraphs
- o Supporting images and videos
- o Author Bio
- o Similar blog posts
- o Newsletter subscription box

What should not be on the Blog Details page:

- o Long blocks of text
- o Confusing headline
- o No social media sharing option

Testimonials Page

A testimonial page is also an incredibly important thing to have on your website. This page is where you can showcase what your clients have to say about you and your services. For new visitors to your website, this page is proof of your excellence and abilities. Hence, you must design it in such a manner that it grabs the attention of the users.

As your business progresses and grows, you will receive testimonials over time. You must choose the best testimonials from among them, and then display them first on the page. Or, if you have served a big company that is quite popular, you might also include their testimonial, as it works to showcase your expertise and greatly increase your credibility and trust.

To make your testimonials look credible and legit, include the real name and a picture of the customer writing the testimonial. If you want to go the extra length with your testimonials, you can also get your customers to record a video testimonial. These are preferred by everyone over common text testimonials.

Image: Sample Testimonial Page

What should be on the Testimonial page:

- o Real names and images of clients
- o Detailed testimonials
- o Video testimonials, if possible
- o Highlight key points in quotes

What should not be on the Testimonial page:

- o Short, 1-2 word testimonials
- o No image or name of the customer
- o Fake testimonials

Case Study Page

A case study is a study done on a person, group of people or a company to showcase your work and attract potential customers and visitors to your website. Through these case studies, users can learn about your offering, and about how you can similarly help them.

Case studies serve to educate customers, drive traffic, and increase conversions of your website. You must keep the customers in mind when you're showcasing a case study. Go for a case study that's industry-specific, rather than being generic, to make sure you address the right customers.

Once you have done that, address the problem that the previous customer had, along with how your service or product helped them to solve that problem. Include the customer's details, to increase the credibility of the study, and include statistics to show how your services can benefit them. This gives a measurable, realistic goal to consumers.

Image: Sample Case Study Page

Include images (whenever possible) to give the study a tremendous boost in visual appeal and a professional look. At the end of the case study, highlight the key takeaway points, and then offer a CTA at the end.

What should be on the Case Study page:

- o A catchy title
- o Client's details
- o Address their problem
- o How your services solved the problem
- o Statistics and evidence
- o Images and video
- o CTA at the end

What should not be on the Case Study page:

- o A fictional case
- o Unnecessary details
- o Picking a random client
- o Complex jargons

Career Page

This is a page where companies list all their job openings - and is often overlooked by many website owners! You don't want to be like them; in fact, you must place a lot of emphasis on this page, as this page drives a lot of traffic as well.

Potential job seekers are going to spend a lot of time on this page, going through the listed job requirements and responsibilities. This increases the overall retention time of the page, which is an important metric for SEO. Google tracks the retention time of websites, and that factors into your rankings.

So, apart from storing the applicant's CV data, this page can work to bring in a lot of traffic to your website. If you list your job openings on LinkedIn, a social media website for professionals, don't allow the candidates to post their applications directly there. Instead, get them to click on your site link to apply. Naturally, this page needs to be designed in a clean, professional manner, to get job applicants to apply for your jobs.

Image: Sample Career Page

What should be on the Career page:

o   Clear job descriptions and requirements

o   Clean page layout

o   Bullet points

o   Use the right keywords

o   CTA button to apply

What should not be on the Career page:

o   Long job descriptions

o   Unnecessary links

o   Excessive graphical elements

Ebook Page:

The ebook page of a website contains all the ebooks published by that website. The design of this page should be simple and focused on presenting the ebooks in an organized manner.

Chronological order is preferred where the newest ebook appears on top. However, the ability to search for ebooks must be present to make it easy for users to find exactly what they're looking for.

They must be able to search via category or genre to narrow down their search. When the user clicks on a particular page, they must be taken to an ebook details page where relevant information about the book must be present.

This includes the title of the ebook and a short description of the ebook. The description must include what topics the ebook will cover and how the reader can benefit from reading it.

Prominent features of the book must be listed in bullet points. Include an image of the ebook cover at the top of this page. To download the book, including a submission form where the user will enter details such as name and email and add a CTA button that says 'download'.

In the right section, you can ask the user to subscribe to your newsletter to get notified of new ebook releases. Also, include a 'Popular Ebooks' section where you will display your most downloaded ebooks and a 'Recent Ebooks' section where the visitors can browse the new ebooks released.

Image: Sample EBook Download Page

What should be on the Ebook page:

- o Ebook title
- o Description of ebook
- o Bullet points
- o Use the right keywords
- o Submission form
- o CTA button to download
- o Ebook suggestions

What should not be on the Ebook page:

- o Download without a submission form
- o No images or details

I would suggest that you go with an experienced web design company that has the experience and skill [Don't forget Royex :)] to design these pages for your website. Your job is to check whether proper implementation has been done or not, using this checklist.

Chapter 8

Tips and Tricks to Generate More

Leads

If lead generation is your ultimate goal, then you should read this chapter carefully. Here, I'm going to go over certain strategies and tips that will help to skyrocket your website leads.

This includes website features that improve user experience and ultimately generate leads, as well as concepts such as repeat customers, retargeting, and free tools. Below, I will discuss and explain how you can use these elements to boost your leads like never before.

Automation Features on Websites

Automation features on a website mean that certain actions are performed without any human intervention. They result from human action, and are a response to that action, generated automatically, to generate a proactive response.

In this section, I will discuss three automation features on websites: abandoned cart emails, sequential email, and auto follow up.

Abandoned Cart Email

Earlier on, you may remember that I mentioned a statistic stating that over 70% of users will abandon their online shopping carts, for various reasons. Of course, 7 out of 10 people leaving your cart without paying can be bad for your business.

So what should you do, if a user just leaves your cart? You can't just sit idle about it. Well, luckily, there is an automated system in place that can convince the user to reconsider their cart, and this is known as the "abandoned cart email".

It is an automated email that goes to the user's email address when they abandon their shopping cart. The great news about this email is that it has an open rate of nearly 50%, compared to the average e-commerce email open rate - which sits quite low, at 15%.

You don't have to email each client that leaves their cart. This system is automated; you just have to set it up once, and then you're done!

How to Create a Great Abandoned Cart Email

To create a great abandoned cart email that will compel the users to get back to their cart and complete the purchase, follow these handy guidelines:

Build a well-crafted subject line

The majority of people will decide to open an email entirely based on the subject line. If the subject line doesn't interest them, then it will end up unopened. So, then, what information should you include in the abandoned cart subject?

- o Company name: Start by mentioning your company name
- o Customer name: Stating their name will grab their attention
- o Friendly tone: Avoid an informal tone, opting instead to go for a friendly one
- o Product name or details: Remind them of the items they left in their cart
- o Urgency: Create a sense of urgency in them to react fast

'Give a clear call-to-action

Add a CTA button or link at the end of the email that will prompt the user to respond to it. The CTA should be clear in what it is asking.

A simple message like "return to your cart" does the trick, and will compel the user to proceed to the cart page.

Show your product

Include product images and descriptions in your email, to remind the user of what they had originally added to their cart before they abandoned it.

Naturally, they may forget what they were shopping for earlier, and if they don't see the product in the mail, then they will simply end up deleting it from their mind, and you will lose out on a potential sale.

Create catchy graphics

The subject, CTA, and email content will convince the user to return to their abandoned cart, but a graphically pleasing email will do wonders in forming a great first impression in the user's mind!

Here's how you can design a good-looking email:

- o Design your email by centering your website's theme, for a consistent look which enhances your branding.
- o Avoid using any stock images. Create your own images, and design them based on their purpose.

- o Choose your colors carefully. Different colors can trigger different responses in our minds, so be sure to use colors that induce happy, positive thoughts.
- o Include animated images and interactive media, to add dynamism and energy to your email.

Create a sense of urgency

Make the user realize what they're missing out on by abandoning their cart. You can create a sense of urgency in the user by doing the following:

- o Letting them know that the item will soon go out of stock due to high demand
- o Letting them know how many others have added this item to their cart
- o Adding a countdown to reserve their cart
- o Letting them know that this item may not be restocked, in the future

Offer alternatives

People can abandon their cart for various reasons – and one of those reasons could simply be that they didn't like the product and that it didn't live up to their initial expectations.

However, they may very well still be interested in alternate products that serve the same purpose! So take advantage of this possibility, and offer them alternatives, whenever you can.

Sequential Email

Sequential emails are also automated emails you can set up for your online business. But what exactly are they?

In essence, sequential emails are a series of emails that are sent out automatically to particular users in your email list. They are sent as a result of action from your user, or after a certain period.

It is action-based, because of triggers like:

o   Browsing behavior
o   Subscribing to your list
o   Shopping cart abandonment
o   Reading or downloading content
o   Buying a product

It can also be time-based when these events occur:

o   When they opt-in
o   30 days after purchase
o   On the anniversary of subscribing

These emails only need to be set up once, and then they run on their own! The process is completely automated. Sequential emails are great for converting website visitors to full-fledged customers, who will then go on to recommend your brand to others as well.

Email sequences are great because they are sent when they will have the most impact on the users. If, for instance, you have a shopper who adds something to their cart and then doesn't purchase it, a series of emails will be sent to them reminding and convincing them to return and make the purchase.

None of this takes any extra effort from the owner's side, as the emails are automated, and you get all the benefits - such as customer retention, improved customer relations, and more sales. No matter what kind of business you run, a sequential email can be a great aid in helping you achieve your business goals.

How to Write a Great Email Sequence

Sequential emails can differ, from business to business, but there are still some general rules that everyone must follow when creating these emails. And those are:

Have a catchy subject line

A catchy subject line will always grab the attention of the reader and make them want to open the email. But don't make it something unpredictable that the user won't expect. For example, if they just subscribe to your newsletter, send an email titled, "Welcome to our newsletter". If you send something confusing to your customers, this will result in them not opening the email.

Explain the reason for your email

The next step is to address the reason why they are receiving this email. Whether it be to welcome them, inform them about a new offer, or remind them of their cart, you should make sure to state this in your email in an obvious manner.

Keep them concise

Avoid long emails containing a lot of content that needs to scroll down, over and over, to read. Instead, keep your emails short and to the point, so that the user gets what you are talking about right away.

Include a clear CTA

Email sequences can only be effective when your reader responds to the mail by taking action. And for them to take this action, you need to offer them a call to action. Whatever action you need them to perform, include a CTA that gets them to it.

Auto-Follow Up

Auto-follow up emails allow you to automatically follow up with your clients when they fail to respond to your emails.

Follow-ups are important because more than 80% of sales are made after at least 5 follow-ups. Sadly, around 45% of people give up after the first rejection, and never attempt to follow up. A whopping 92% give up right before the all-important fifth follow-up, and miss out on the sale they were so close to achieving.

Now that you realize the importance of sending follow-ups, keep in mind that these are also time-consuming and that you have to track every email and set up an appropriate email response.

Luckily, however, there are tools and software available that allow you to follow up with your clients automatically. These can be set up once, and all the responses can be pre-written, saved, and then sent out at an appropriate time.

What Type of Event Triggers an Auto Follow Up Email?

- o **When a customer makes a purchase:** Whenever a prospective customer buys something from your website, an automated follow up can be sent to them.
- o **When a product is shipped:** Upon successful order delivery, a follow-up message can be sent to them.

o **When checkout is abandoned:** I discussed this above in the abandoned cart section, but you can easily follow up with messages when they leave out the checkout process abruptly.

What Type of Auto Follow Up Emails Can You Set Up?

o **Feedback:** Obtain valuable feedback from customers that will give you insight into various aspects of your business. You can ask customers about their shopping experience, and whether they would like to do business with you again.

o **Discount:** Offer automated discounts to customers who are of high value to you. You can also offer discounts to customers who haven't shopped with you in a while.

o **Product Recommendations:** Send automated recommendations of products and services. These can be suggestions for items that can be bought together, or you can inform them of new products.

o **Abandoned Checkout:** Automated emails to recover the lost sale, when your customer leaves their shopping cart without checking out. Keep following up until they change their mind.

o **Content:** Send users content, such as blogs and articles that are curated specifically to drive sales.

Generate More Leads by Enhancing User Experience (UX)

So you've created a website to sell your products/services, and you even get a lot of visitors to your site. But are you concerned that you are not being able to convert those visitors to leads? This defeats the whole purpose of a business, where the aim is to increase sales and achieve growth.

In this section, you're going to learn how leads are generated from a website, the importance of UX in lead generation, and how you can generate leads by improving the UI and UX of your website.

How are Leads Generated From a Website?

Here, I will describe the process through which a visitor is turned into a lead is called the "lead generation process", and is described below:

Discovery: Let's say you own a website that sells mobile app development services. A business owner realizes the importance of having a mobile app and is interested in developing a mobile app for his business.

He searches the internet with the query "best mobile app developer". He then discovers your website from there, and this is how he's found you. A visitor might also find you via your social channels, or through a video.

Information assessment: The business owner then goes through the content of your website, analyzing the services and features you offer. He is then greeted with a call-to-action (CTA) button that, once clicked, will take him to a landing page. If the visitor is impressed by your content and your website design, he will then click on the CTA button and proceed to the landing page.

Sign-up: The landing page will offer the visitor something that is of value to them – and to access this offered content, the user must fill out a form, in which he provides basic information, such as his name and email. This is a win-win situation for both parties, as they get their valued content, and you have successfully generated a lead, thus completing the customer's journey from a visitor to a customer.

Why Does UX Matter For Lead Generation?

If you are wondering whether User Experience plays any role in lead generation, then let me tell you that both are closely related. Lead generation greatly depends on the website's user experience. If a user is not satisfied with navigating your website, they will just leave and go to another one.

UX leaves a very strong first impression on the minds of the visitors, and it can either break or make your business. Let's discuss some reasons why User Experience is such a prerequisite for lead generation:

To avoid confusion: Although there are many modern and really interesting ways to build a website, they are not all perfect for the user. Forcing someone to try out a complicated new interface, just because you want to be special, is a real risk. You don't want the visitors to leave your website out of confusion.

Increased Return on Investment (ROI): It has been proven that, if you invest in a solid, profitable UX strategy, your ROI increases significantly:

- There's $100 in return for every dollar invested in UX - that's a 9,900% ROI.
- A $10,000 investment in design-centric companies will yield a 228% greater return than the same investment in S&P in 10 years.
- 86% of customers are willing to spend more for better customer experience.

Decreased bounce rate: Does UX affect your site's bounce rate?

You bet it does! UX, when done well, can substantially lower the bounce rate for your website! The numbers speak for themselves:

- o Due to poor user experience, 89% of customers stopped doing business with a rival.
- o When photos don't load (or take too long to load), 39% of people will stop interacting with a website.
- o 47% of people hope that a website will load in 2 seconds or less.
- o The bounce rate at Time.com dropped 15% after continuous scrolling was introduced.

Impact of design on lead generation: Think you can throw around a few colors on your website, and the users will just love it? Well, not quite. The website design should be well-thought-out and studied, to see what people are responding to positively. Design impacts the user experience much more than you think; let these figures prove the point:

- o First impressions are 94% design-related.
- o After a bad experience, 88% of online users are less likely to return to the site.
- o Site reputation assessments are 75% dependent on the overall design.
- o If the interface is unattractive, 38% of users will stop interacting with a website.

Mobile Optimization matters: People nowadays are on their phone screens constantly. This ensures that, when they visit your website, there is a high possibility that it's going to be from their mobile devices.

Getting your site mobile-optimized may seem like no big deal, but the honest fact is that it can make an enormous difference. Optimizing a mobile site should be your top priority because:

- o 74% of people are more likely to return to a site when it is mobile-optimized.
- o 67% of mobile users say that they are more likely to buy a product or service from a website when the website is mobile-friendly.
- o Because of a bad mobile experience, 52% of consumers are less likely to engage with a business.

Tips and Tricks to Improve Your Website's User Experience

Your website is the fundamental pillar of your digital marketing efforts. One key aspect of designing a great experience for website users requires knowing the problems that various visitors tend to face.

Far more than ever before, your website is a powerful tool in today's marketing landscape. Your website is a 24/7 salesperson, and therefore, it can very well prove to be your most potent tool and the centerpiece of all your marketing efforts.

Rapidly-evolving digital trends, however, can also make your website feel pretty outdated. And while a redesign may sometimes be necessary, you might not have the time or resources to engage in such a major project.

"Your website is a 24/7 salesperson, and therefore, it can very well prove to be your most potent tool and the centerpiece of all your marketing efforts."

To help you conquer this challenge, we have compiled a list of 10 easy ways to make your website more functional and productive. These tips will ultimately result in improved lead generation, and your business will be booming.

1. Utilize whitespace

Whitespace is imperative for a well-designed website. It makes the content more readable, while also allowing the user to concentrate on the elements that accompany the text. White space can also increase user attention by more than 20%.

By implementing white space, you can make your website feel connected, new, and up-to-date - and if the branding is compatible with these, it can also allow you to convey this feeling to the user. Nevertheless, one downside to bear in mind about white space is that it takes up space.

The key is to find the balance between what's most important for sharing at the top, and then surrounding that with some space to help illustrate the image and/or text.

2. Minimize your page loading times

One of the most unpleasant experiences for web users is waiting too long for a page to load. With the rise of mobile devices, people all over the world are now able to access content on many different platforms. Whether it be online browsing or watching TV on their laptop, they expect an immediate response to the content they are looking for.

Generally, when they don't get a quick response, they bounce. Slow page loading can be a source of frustration, and users often just don't have the time or the inclination to wait. An additional five seconds of page loading time can increase the "bounce rate" of your website by more than 20%.

3. Make use of appealing CTA buttons

Customers already have a habit of following visual indications to evaluate which content is essential to them. Calls to action (CTAs) that are clearly labeled with a word for action enable users of your website to navigate your site more easily and to get exactly what they want, in the area they expect to find it in.

You should think about color and the psychology of color when creating buttons for your website. Different colors trigger different signals. Consider the image you want to elicit for a customer (confidence, knowledge, intelligence) and then carefully choose your colors accordingly.

4. Make your hyperlinks stand out

If you add a link to any page, you're saying that you want the user to click on it. Make sure your links are easily visually identifiable. Underlined text, and text that is colored differently, attract the viewer's attention and let them know that this is a link to click on.

Knowing user preferences, and what they already know about web usage, is the key to success. Stop thinking about the length of the hyperlink while hyperlinking, as well. The longer the names of the links are, the easier they are to recognize.

5. Highlight key information using bullet points

Bullet points will allow the user to understand what they want to know quickly: the ways you can fix their problem, as well as the specifications of a product/service - all within a very short timeframe. This will make your points more appealing and will encourage your customers to easily access all the information they need.

You can also get artistic with your bullet points by customizing the icon design, and inspire the reader with images that reflect your argument.

6. Make the most of the images on your website

Users today have become way more intelligent at browsing websites. With only a glance, they can decide if they would like to proceed further. Therefore, making a solid first impression with your website is vital.

If they're visiting your site for the first time, they can easily spot a generic stock picture that they have already seen elsewhere, or that is close to the non-personal style of stock photography.

The use of stock photography will reduce trust - not to mention stand out as common and non-unique. And such partnerships sadly do carry over to your company. Another thing you should consider is getting a high-quality logo design, to make your brand stand out!

7. Optimize your headings

Everything your potential customers are searching for should dictate your headings and posts. It's also very important to include keywords in your title so that you target your message and attract the right audience.

Search engines usually give more weight to headings over other content, so you can significantly improve your search capabilities just by choosing the right heading and making it stand out.

8. Maintain uniformity in your website

Consistency means doing everything in a way that it aligns with each other. This includes heading sizes, choices of type, shading, key designs, arrangement, elements of architecture, types of illustration, choices of images, etc. To make the template cohesive between pages and on the same page, everything should be theme-set.

Drastic changes in design from page to page will cause your user to feel confused and lost, and they will quickly lose confidence in your website. According to the consumer, design irregularities lower the quality of the products and services you are offering.

9. Find and fix 404 errors on your site

Although search engines do not severely punish you for soft 404 errors ("page not found"), a user will. Whenever a user encounters a link or a picture, they expect this connection to take them to the next place they want to go.

Simply put, having a 404 error page irritates the user, and makes them think twice about spending their time on your website (when they could go for a more reliable alternative elsewhere).

Running into 404s is another incredibly irritating occurrence for a customer, right next to poor page load time, and it disrupts their flow through the website.

10. Ensure responsiveness and mobile-friendliness

Websites are an important part of this evolution, too. A website must be mobile-friendly and easy-to-use, irrespective of what type of device people are using to access it.

Google has recently started to penalize pages that aren't designed for mobile devices, making the need for accessibility even more important than ever. Perhaps this is the single most valuable way to improve the performance of your website.

We hope these tips will help you improve the UX of your website.

Repeat Customers

One common mistake businesses make is attempting to increase their revenue is spending their time and budget on acquiring new customers.

It's great to expand your business by increasing your customer base, of course, but it's not the most optimal use of your time and budget. Instead, you can shift your focus to the most valuable resource: your existing customers.

> *"'80% of profits come from 20% of customers'.*
> *These 20% are your existing customers, and you*
> *should focus on retaining them."*

Concentrating on customer retention and enabling repeat customers is far more effective in creating long term, profitable relationships. Here's why:

- o **Repeat customers spend more money:** Repeat customers spend 300% more than new customers, according to a study. They bring in more revenue, and they trust your products and services.

o **Repeat customers are easier to sell to:** As they trust you more than new customers do, it is much easier to convince and sell to them. On average, you have a 13% chance to convince new customers and, in comparison, a 60%-70% chance of selling to repeat customers.

o **Repeat customers promote your business:** Marketing can be extremely expensive for small businesses, but if you have repeat customers, they will promote your business for free! They are likely to refer to 50% more people than new customers are.

o **Businesses are built on customer retention:** We all know the famous Pareto principle which states, "80% of profits come from 20% of customers". These 20% are your existing customers, and you should focus on retaining them.

How to Get More Repeat Customers to Your Website

Encourage New Customers to Register an Account

Asking new customers to register an account during the checkout process can make their checkout process harder, and 23% of users will leave their carts behind if they are being compelled to create an account.

But outside of the checkout process, you can ask them to create an account and register with your website. You can even explain that it is a one-time process and that it will make their shopping experience better when they make a purchase next time.

Now that you have their email, you can send them emails informing them about all the latest offers, products and discounts that are exclusive only to members.

Offer Incentives and Loyalty Programs

Offer a special discount for first-time buyers, to give them the incentive to purchase again. You can also send out discount codes via email that have an expiry date attached to them, to add a sense of urgency.

For long-term customers, reward them with a loyalty program that grants them unique and special perks, to make them feel valued and appreciated.

Ask for Feedback

When customers are done shopping, you can ask for their feedback about their shopping experience. Ask them what they felt was great about it, and what needs improving.

You can gather this feedback either via a star rating or a survey, in which they can answer certain questions.

This feedback can help you further improve your customer experience and, eventually, it will help you retain customers.

Showcase Customer Social Media Posts

Customers often post photos of them using your product. Collect these posts and publish them on your website in a curated manner; and you can show them on your social media, as well!

This will promote your business brand, increase your sales, and retain existing customers. Your brand gets valuable exposure at no extra cost.

Retargeting

Retargeting also referred to as remarketing, is a way of re-engaging customers who interacted with your website and left without converting. To re-engage them, ads on your website are shown to them when they visit other websites.

The ads follow them around the internet. Retargeting works better than other ads because they are targeting people who have already visited your site. They know about what you are offering, and this reminder in the form of an ad may be just the thing that brings them back to your website.

Retargeting has proven to be effective in increasing the chances of sales that had previously been thought of as lost opportunities.

How Does Retargeting Work?

Retargeting works by placing cookies on your site that track the users who have visited your site. Depending on the ad service that you use, your ads will be displayed on their network. For example, if you use Google, it will display your ad on all the sites that are a part of Google's AdSense program.

Ads can either be pay-per-click (PPC) or cost-per-impression (CPM), with the former charging for clicks on ads, and the latter charging based on impressions.

You can start with a small budget, and see how well retargeting works for you. If it increases your ROI, you can then increase your budget on it. If done right, retargeting will be able to bring back a bunch of lost sales from visitors who have left your site.

Free Tools

Offering free tools and incentives on your website is an excellent way to increase traffic and conversions.

If you offer freebies regularly on your website, people will return for more. Eventually, the site will rank faster in search engines, and your sales will skyrocket!

The usual technique for offering these free tools is to get the users to enter their email to avail of the free download.

Once they've filled out the form, you now have their email address, which you can then add to your contact list and periodically send them emails on new products, offers, downloads, etc.

These freebies are a powerful lead magnet, and what you offer will naturally depend on the type of business that you run. Common tools include:

- Ebooks
- Webinars
- Design & Templates
- Lists and roundups
- Workbooks
- Training videos
- Calculators
- E-courses
- Source Code
- Coupons & discount codes

Conclusion

Let me summarize here what I've tried to explain throughout these past pages. If you search online, you will find several tips to make your website generate leads. It is easy to follow tips… and it's even easier to write those tips.

But in all reality, a great lead generating website cannot be developed that simply. You need to understand your service, your buyers, your buyer's behaviors, how your buyer navigates your website, how you can please your buyer, and why your buyer will contact you.

"Remember that lead generation is a slow process that takes time and patience"

You need to know all the details. Your buyer's behavior may be very different from my buyer's behavior, for instance. So, your website design and your buyer's journey on the website should be different from that of my buyer's journey. That's why you need to understand the whole concept before you set about redesigning your website.

I based the whole design process centered around the buyer's behavior and their journey. Each buyer behavior and the journey is unique, and you cannot simply generalize buyer behavior by analyzing a few visitors.

This is why we develop buyer personas to understand their needs. Serving customers based on their needs is the most effective way of converting them – and this is precisely why I dedicated the entire first two chapters of this book to getting to know your buyers and understanding their behavior.

The mistake that most businesses make is that they aim for the most visually appealing website, but forget to ever consider and factor their buyers into their design process. This is one of the biggest mistakes you can make because it is the buyers that you are even making the website for in the first place.

The buyer's journey is a three-stage process, in which they go through awareness, consideration, and decision. In the fifth chapter, I described how you can create content for each stage of the buyer's journey, to improve your chances of getting them to convert.

Knowing where your buyers come from will also help you to optimize your website accordingly. A buyer who has arrived at your website by directly typing your website into their address bar will naturally act and behave differently than someone who comes from your social media pages.

In essence, the source of traffic dictates their navigational behavior, so the goal is to build your website keeping that in mind. In chapter 6, I showed you exactly that, listing out website redesign strategies based on your source of traffic.

So you need to combine all the information of your buyer, and then finally begin designing your website to achieve the best possible results. Once you have done that, you can make other tweaks and changes to further optimize your website for lead generation.

Basically, through this book, I've tried to make you knowledgeable enough to design your website perfectly, which can then go on to generate leads.

Remember that lead generation is a slow process, that takes time and patience. All the information I have shared in this book comes as a result of my 17 years of experience in the field of website design and development.

I sincerely hope that after reading this book, you will be able to implement these ideas and build a website that functions as a lead magnet for you and brings you success like never before.

If you have any queries related to any topics inside this book, please don't hesitate to contact me! Just drop an email to rajib@royex.net, and I will try and answer all your questions.

If you feel that you need my direct consultancy for your website redesign, please let me know.

About the Author

"You can't connect the dots looking forward; you can only connect them looking backward. So you have to trust that the dots will somehow connect in your future…" — *Steve Jobs*

Rajib Roy (1980-) is a software developer, entrepreneur, and author who was born in Chittagong, Bangladesh. He attained a Bachelor's in Electrical and Electronic Engineering from Chittagong University of Engineering and Technology and a Master's in Computer Engineering from Herriot Watt University. Today, Rajib lives in Dubai, with his wife and his two sons.

In his day job, Rajib runs his own software company, with branches in Dubai, India, and Bangladesh. He has been instrumental in the start-up of several businesses and been responsible for building several projects which are now running successfully in different enterprises, more than 400 websites, 50 Mobile apps, and several Enterprise Systems.

Having always had an interest in technology, Rajib has written more than 100 articles for technical journals and websites. Now, however, he has taken a bigger step, with his first book, *Turn Your Website Into a Lead Machine*, which is now available through Amazon.

In his spare time, Rajib spends much of it with his family, but he is also heavily interested in technology, and enjoys photography and reading, usually getting through 4 to 5 books per month.

As far as the future is concerned, Rajib wants to become someone who leaves a lasting impression by changing the society he lives in with ever-greater advances in technology. He may also continue to write more books and articles.

You can contact or follow Rajib Roy at the following:

Website - https://www.mrroy.info

Twitter - https://twitter.com/rkroy

LinkedIn - https://www.linkedin.com/in/rkroy/

Email - rajib@royex.net

About Royex Technologies

In Feb. 2013, I decided to establish a software development firm to support my existing business. Initially, the Royex team only worked for those companies, but after a few years, we decided to work directly for local clients. In the beginning, we were only designing websites, but we eventually began providing 12 different services, and we now have more than 25 readymade products for clients.

Our initial target was to provide the best support and product at a limited cost. That's why we established our development office in India and Bangladesh, but our sales office is in Dubai. We employed over 50 people across these three locations. By maintaining the minimum number of employees in Dubai, we can keep our costs and prices lower than our competitors. Even so, because our support team is in Dubai, our customers can still enjoy face-to-face meetings and explain their vision clearly. This is just one way that we can provide great service with minimum cost. Moreover, our online support system can easily provide our clients with trackable support.

We have experience in working with small- to large-sized corporations, from startups to big corporate giants.

Our Services:

- Mobile App Development Company Dubai
- Website Development
- Search Engine Optimization
- eCommerce Web Design Dubai
- Custom Application Development
- Magento Development
- Umbraco Development
- WordPress Development
- AWS Consulting and Maintenance
- Security and Vulnerability Testing
- Branding and Logo Design

Website:

https://www.royex.ae

INDEX